THE PRACTICE OF MINISTRY

Preparing to Navigate the Unknown

CAROL PINKHAM OAK

Church PUBLISHING

Church Publishing
19 East 34th Street
New York, NY 10016
www.churchpublishing.org

Cover design by Newgen
Typeset by Nord Compo

ISBN 978-1-64065-880-6 (paperback)
ISBN 978-1-64065-881-3 (eBook)

Library of Congress Control Number: 2026943715

In Memory of the Right Reverend Robert Rae Spears Jr.,
fifth bishop of Rochester, 1918-2008,
the first mentor to ask, "What did you learn?"

TABLE OF CONTENTS

INTRODUCTION

Preparing to navigate the unknown—and beginning my adventure with my future self as the founder of a consulting organization for mentoring and peer learning called Soul Assets—started the day my husband Jeff said to me, "We have to get a life!" Our two children were in college, there were no ministry or job transitions on the horizon for either of us, and the dog was healthy and middle-aged. That frantic stage of life known as being a parent of school-aged kids was rapidly sinking below the horizon. We needed another sun to come up.

Long conversations followed about our emerging stage of life. We recognized that we had the benefit of flexibility, even though we were not yet completely untethered from our immediate family's schedules. We talked about our foundational values, which included restorative time with friends and family centered around our love of cooking with local foods and making time for play—being active beneath the sun and surrounded by saltwater.

Sailing topped this "playlist." Fundamentally, sailing requires setting a point of navigation on the horizon and then using the dynamic energy of wind, waves, tides, sails, rudder, and the sailor's skill to navigate a course to that chosen point. All the elements are continually changing. The sailor tracks the shifting conditions and adjusts, sometimes rapidly and with vigor, sometimes more leisurely and with less effort. We decided we could best describe our current stage of life as one defined by adjusting along a spectrum from vigorous to little effort.

We soon purchased a classic day sailor, a Herreshoff 12½. For those unfamiliar with sailboats, a Herreshoff 12½ is a boat designed in 1912 for young sailors learning in the brisk conditions of the bays off Cape Cod. If you know next to nothing about sailing, think of a day sailor as a boat that is comfortable enough to sit in for a long afternoon but too small to sleep in overnight. And, for those unfamiliar with nautical terms, boats are traditionally referred to as "she." Sensing she would console the apprehension and unease that we both felt in our souls as our identities as parents changed, and knowing she could transport us out of our familiar harbor and stay steadfast as we tested the unfamiliar waters of our next life stage, we named the boat *Soul Asset.*

The ministry I practice now is also called "Soul Assets." Using the plural of the second word intentionally, Soul Assets combines Connection, Clarity, and Momentum into a complementary set of tools to navigate the stages and contexts of daily life for spiritual leaders. With over thirty-nine years of ordained ministry in The Episcopal

Church, I have learned about our Connection to God, to ourselves, and to others. I have tested how to gain Clarity around foundational questions and issues. And I have discovered that with Connection and Clarity around today's questions, Momentum builds for tomorrow's actions.

Like wind, waves, and tides that change and shift each time I set sail aboard *Soul Asset*, I have come to see that the energy behind Connection, Clarity, and Momentum also changes and shifts. When combined, the energy generated by Connection, Clarity, and Momentum propels the metaphorical ship of spiritual leadership to the desired point.

In fact, I believe that Connection, Clarity, and Momentum are foundational for leadership development in *any* field. While the terminology describing these three elements might vary from profession to profession—how its core tenets are described in modules or on checklists—any conversation about leadership reveals that Connection, Clarity, and Momentum are key to developing specific leadership skills.

Classroom leadership curricula or programs that focus only on concepts miss that vital element that integrates Connection, Clarity, and Momentum: learning from individual experience in context. Learning from experience does not entail simply participating in an experience and then individually determining what you learned from it. Although it is tempting to focus solely on the experience itself to determine what knowledge is gained, to me, that approach risks missing crucial discoveries and the depth of learning.

Instead, I believe that to truly learn from experience, one must intentionally choose an experience that is part of one's vocational context and then, employing focused questions and thoughtful conversation partners, reflect on what one has learned from that experience within that specific context. Only this reflective approach fosters the type of knowledge that can be applied to the leader's next spiritual leadership experience.

To return to the sailing metaphor, a sailor's navigational knowledge and skill expand and deepen each day as the energy of wind, waves, tides, and sun shifts. The navigational skills and knowledge sailors possess each time they board their vessel to embark on a particular day's voyage must adjust to the conditions encountered on the water. So too, the skill and knowledge possessed by a leader must be expanded on a particular day as they navigate the "waters" of human activity. True, fundamental principles absorbed from training or a curriculum provide a solid foundation. Learning from direct experience in context, however, integrates this more academic knowledge with a leader's "real life" experience in their context and vocation.

The aim of this book is to create a navigational chart for the spiritual leader through their direct experience of ministry leadership. To support this new type of learning experience, the book describes the natural, dynamic elements of Connection, Clarity, and

Momentum and explains how leaders may nurture these elements to continually improve their ministry practice. These pages include accounts of current experience in professional practice, particularly ministry practice. I will also provide exercises for personal, vocational, and professional growth, and provide a guide for engaging in reflective practice—a reflection process using direct experience of ministry practice as an essential tool to growth, insight, and moving forward—and share a tested framework within which intentional reflective practice conversations take place. My goal is to encourage the reader to develop a personal reflective habit supported by participation in a learning community, a habit that inspires ongoing growth and a new identity as a reflective practitioner in ministry.

Soul Assets Consulting brings together all the resources to learn and to practice the exercises, conversation models, and the reflective practice process in this book. These resources are the result of twenty-six years of ministry mentoring clergy at all different stages and contexts of ministry and forming learning communities.

Learning in Community

Typically, a learning community of reflective practitioners comprises six to ten participants who find themselves asking similar questions because they have reached a similar stage in their ministry experience. For example, a learning community could be comprised of those in the initial five years of ordained ministry. Alternatively, a learning community could be established for lay leaders within a congregation who are discerning the significance of signals of change in their surrounding community for the church, mission, or neighborhood organization and how they might need to innovate in response. A learning community could also take the form of a practice group of lay preachers, formation leaders, or staff in similar positions across dioceses. In short, learning communities form around the context, questions, and needs of the participants.

Although a solo reader can certainly use the reflection questions and learning community templates found in this book, inspiring a solo voyage is not my intent in writing this book. Again, to use the sailing metaphor, children often learn to sail on a small craft known as Sunfish sailbots. These are low, surfboard-like boats with a single sail, ideally suited for young or beginning sailors to learn everything they need to know about navigating a boat—provided the skies are sunny and the breezes moderate. During their childhoods on the water, our kids sailed with other kids.

As the adults in the appointed safety boats, we towed many a Sunfish, captained by one of the kids, to safety after the wind picked up, the sky turned deep gray, and the waves became too powerful for the little boat and its crew of frightened sailors. To be fair, even an extraordinarily skilled adult could not successfully sail a Sunfish to shore in those conditions, because it is not designed to maneuver effectively in rough seas. Larger boats, of course, can contend with volatile weather, though they are also more complicated to sail. More significantly, larger sailboats require more than one sailor. (Yes, I know. A well-traveled, experienced sailor is getting ready to write to me about how they managed a ninety-foot boat single-handed in gale-force winds. Well done! That sort of exceptional skill and extreme conditions, however, are beyond the purview of this book.)

I therefore encourage prospective readers to form a learning group. Why? Because learning from experience requires multiple perspectives. We all possess blind spots. We all have a particular view of ourselves that others may not share. We see only what we can see at a given moment. Learning from experience in context happens in the rich, complex, dynamic conversation that I advocate *only within community.* Community members hear from multiple perspectives, discuss questions together, learn about different scenarios and contexts, and generally support one another. These elements of practice create conditions so that each member of the community feels both safe and confident about making the adjustments needed to reach their desired destination as leaders.

I write as a practicing Christian. I believe a life in Christ means continually growing, evolving, and reforming as we live in our present world. In John 15:15, Jesus tells his disciples, "I have called you friends, because I have made known to you everything that I have heard from my Father." With these words, Jesus empowers us to enter into an active relationship with him, acknowledges our agency, and calls each of us into our own action. We do not choose the era into which we are born, but we can choose how we live faithfully in our time on earth to make Christ known and to respect the dignity of every human being. I encourage readers to adapt the stories and words herein to their own faith tradition, whatever it may be. That way, you will practice what is most active and most true to you.

I also encourage readers to appreciate the church as a hierarchical organization with dynamics similar to other professional organizations. There are accountabilities, responsibilities, roles, boundaries, and expectations among all people in an organization so that the mission of that organization can be accomplished. There are sound financial practices, employment laws, pension obligations, and payroll controls common to other organizations where employees are paid. Many of the examples I use are drawn from church contexts. I define those so readers can translate the insights into their own context. Spiritual leaders serve everywhere.

The scenarios that open most chapters are drawn from actual experiences within The Episcopal Church. And the dynamics in these scenarios could happen in any hierarchical organization. To help the reader understand terms unique to Episcopal churches:

- A parish is a congregation.
- A priest is analogous to a pastor or minister.
- A curate is new to ministry and a new hire.
- The rector is an experienced clergyperson and leads the congregation.
- The bishop oversees all the parishes and clergy in a specific geographic region.
- The Commission on Ministry advises the bishop concerning those seeking ordination as deacons or priests.

I write as a leader grounded in the life of the church. I encourage readers from other organizational settings to take what is useful and adapt it to their own contexts. To translate these scenarios into a business context, the analogous roles are: curate → new hire, rector → supervisor, and bishop → chief executive.

However, because the mission of the church is to make Christ known, the church is different from a business. Church dynamics are more complex, I believe, because we cannot completely rely on a rule, or a law, or a policy, or a chief executive officer's personality for final guidance. We rely on our practice of continually reflecting on our experiences of bringing together theology, scripture, good business practices, the needs of human dignity, prayer, the reasonable boundaries of community, and leadership insight. In this complexity, there is never one formula to determine an answer.

My wish for readers is that all will be inspired to sail their own boats using a new set of navigational tools, honed for the unique waters of your ministry.

The journey begins: To launch our leadership adventure, chapter 1 outlines the fundamentals of *Connection* that are distinct for Christian leaders in congregations and for anyone seeking to grow as a spiritual leader in any organization. Connection describes our deepening relationship with God, ourselves, and one another. As a Christian, I abide by Matthew's words: "You shall love the Lord your God with all your heart, and with all your soul, and with all your mind." This is the greatest and first commandment. And the second is like it: "You shall love your neighbor as yourself" (Matthew 22: 37-39). Connection encompasses self-awareness, inner prayer life, and relationships that hold lessons currently difficult for us to uncover. An event, quandary, unanticipated exchange, or insight in one of these areas is an experience for reflection. Especially in the multidimensional contexts of ministry, *clarity* improves understanding and is the subject of chapter 2. In my experience, there is often reluctance to do the hard work required to gain real clarity, due to an understandable desire to be softer or more pastoral. The sharper the image our conversation partners and we can develop, the greater the number of potential approaches.

Combining the connection described in chapter 1 with the clarity described in chapter 2 opens the way for the momentum to move. Connection and clarity together generate the potential for momentum, a positive energy for what is possible, for deciding on concrete actions, and for accountability of the members of the learning community. Chapter 2 describes ways to gain clarity and gather momentum.

Chapter 3 covers the background, learning theory, and guiding principles of reflective practice. Reflective practice and becoming a reflective practitioner require learning from experience in context. The reader engages this chapter's exercises, generating new knowledge to apply to ministry. This is a new learning process in the profession of ministry. This chapter offers a vocabulary for learning community conversations and provides a template for using experience as the content of learning.

The stages of ministry practice are described in chapter 4. A spiritual leader's stage of ministry practice influences how they navigate the complex and dynamic ministry issues they encounter. The chapter specifically describes these stages and outlines an initial framework for developing lay spiritual leadership as a springboard for conversation and innovation.

Chapter 5 identifies the catalyst for focused learning communities—namely, experienced clergy trained in facilitating the learning process, who have become reflective practitioners and serve as mentors not only for community conversations but also for individuals in the learning community. The mentor's ministry is woven into the hearts of the members as everyone learns with and from one another.

Next, chapter 6 explores the potential of classical seminary education and examines its acceptable limits. The chapter invites us to let go of once and for all the familiar phrase, "I didn't learn that in seminary." Theological education is not supposed to teach us everything an ordained spiritual leader needs to know for the practice of ministry. We are active practitioners in our own ministry development, rather than simply passive recipients of what is offered during our initial theological education. The chapter invites the reader to ask, "What is the next learning platform?" "What does the practice of continuous learning look like?" "What are the skills that are normal for a certain stage of ministry practice?"

All changes involve the grief of letting go of what is familiar. This letting go includes the stages of our own vocational identity that we carefully built in the past and that now no longer serve us. Accepting the natural limits of theological education enables us to set sail as reflective practitioners.

We now board a sailboat that will traverse the waters by learning from the experiences of navigating the changing conditions and challenges. Learning from direct experience within ministry and other professional contexts is known as reflective practice. The elements of reflective practice come together in the same way a sailor, as the captain of a boat, engages the conditions of wind, water, and skill in moment-by-moment adjustments to keep the boat sailing in the desired direction. To learn how to engage the elements of reflective practice, exercises, reflection questions, scenarios, and case stories are offered. Welcome to this learning journey in the practice of ministry as we prepare to navigate the unknown in our own contexts of changing conditions and challenges.

CHAPTER 1

Connection

No one would live in Boston without owning a winter coat. But countless people think they can exercise leadership without partners.

—Ron Heiftz, a saying well-known
from his lectures on leadership
at the Harvard Kennedy School.

The newly arrived rector attended her first clergy gathering. Curious to get to know her new colleagues, she started a conversation with one of the longest-serving clergy in the area. At the end of the meeting, he invited her to lunch. When he suggested a date, she responded, "That is my day off. Can we pick another time?" Her senior colleague responded, "Rectors never get a day off."

The pastor was totally surprised the first time it happened during his first year of ministry. Years later, however, the random occurrences were a welcome "surprise." Once or twice a year, always on a beautiful day, a member of his governing board would arrive at his office door with a picnic basket. "Greetings, Pastor! It is a beautiful day. We have taken care of the rest of the afternoon. Your spouse also has the afternoon off. Please enjoy the lovely day together." A few days later, a colleague asked the pastor, "Do you think you will ever move to another congregation?" "Never," he replied.

Both the stories relayed above are real-life clergy experiences. Together, they illustrate the full spectrum of *connection*—from profound engagement to complete disconnection.

At one extreme lies isolation—both from others and from oneself. When no connection exists to yourself within your heart, and no connection exists to others, then any connection to God is likely to constitute little more than going through the ritual motions. What connection exists is abstract, generating little warmth.

At the opposite end of the spectrum, as shown in the second account, is a relationship with congregational leadership that fosters connection rather than isolation, benefiting both the staff and the congregation. Such a connection can occur when all involved are clear about the roles of the governing board and the pastor, the need for pastoral care of a pastor, and when and how to show appreciation and friendship for a leader. It is important to note that the congregation's offer of these spiritual gifts is not because the pastor requests or earns them, but because the congregation intentionally seeks to model the self-giving love of God—in the form of a picnic basket. Unfortunately, the dynamic between pastor and parish relayed in the first story is a more common occurrence than that relayed in the second.

An extraordinarily difficult condition for sailors is being in "irons": the wind has died, and therefore the boat has no power to move. Both the boat and the sailor are stuck until the wind picks up again. Being in irons is like loneliness. As I have listened to clergy, both those in their initial years of ministry and those with years of experience, I hear most often how alone they feel. Yet only occasionally are the words, "I am lonely," spoken directly. More often, the leader says, "I tried starting the conversation in the vestry," or "My wardens do not see the need to look ahead three years," or "There is no one else I can talk to about this" (even when the "this" is not misconduct).

Such admissions represent a very real dynamic in ministry practice. One cause of this type of clergy loneliness could be that the emotional layers and relationships within the congregation are so interwoven that literally no one exists with whom it is safe to discuss a delicate issue. It might be that faithful vestry members fail to connect the impact that another vestry leader's actions can have on the congregation. Friendships and loyalties are entangled in complex cross-purposes. Under these conditions, the priest often must deal with the issue alone.

Similarly, if key leadership seeks to maintain the status quo in worship, programming, pastoral care, and vestry meetings at the expense of identifying what might need to change in the future, the spiritual leader can feel like he or she is leading alone. In congregations with a single trained/ordained spiritual leader, the options for conferring with colleagues who completely understand your context are limited. And let's not forget how easy it is for clergy to get stuck in "isn't it awful" conversations in which everything that is conceivably wrong in the parish is itemized: the members, the budget, the bishop, the allotment—anything that makes parish life uncomfortable. These conversations feel lonely to clergy because, in "isn't it awful" mode, everyone is generating negativity. No one is connecting. The wind has died. The sailor and the boat are stuck.

It is not only clergy who are lonely. Recently, researchers have described a loneliness epidemic in other human contexts. College campuses are often described as being rife with loneliness. The expectation is that college students naturally talk with one another about classes, sports, politics, arts, and all the rich, diverse perspectives they encounter on their campuses. Yet professors report that their students ask them how to have a conversation with another person.

Heather Holleman, an associate professor at Penn State University, authored a book for her students, *The Six Conversations: Pathways to Connecting in an Age of Isolation and Incivility.* In it, she identifies a foundational principle for conversation-seeking students: to be curious about other people. Then she suggests they ask a question based on any one of the six dimensions that make us human: social, physical, emotional, cognitive, volitional, or spiritual.[1]

Connecting Conversations

Clearly, the first step to connection is conversation. Once a conversation has started, some kind of connection is formed. Susan Scott, author of *Fierce Conversations* (Berkley Books, 2004), declares that a pillar of meaningful conversations is recognizing that the conversation is the relationship. She calls these "fierce" conversations—strong, intentional, with the potential to change a life, a career, or a direction. The core of the conversation is the relationship; however, if you are not talking to someone meaningfully, you are not forming a relationship. Short bursts of small talk, texts, polite conversations with someone in a social setting that you may or may not see again, are not a relationship.

I recall an attempt at conversation to form a relationship when I was in the early days of a new call. A senior leader asked me in a very perfunctory tone, "So, how's the family?" I thought the question odd since at that point he had not met my two teenagers, who were away at school. I could also tell from his tone that he was checking a social box. He was not genuinely curious about me and therefore not interested in my answer. He

1. Heather Holleman, *The Six Conversations: Pathways to Connecting in an Age of Isolation and Incivility* (Moody Publishers, 2022).

also had no interest in an intentional conversation, a direction for the conversation, or any kind of exchange that might bring about change. This conversation was a closer rather than one that led to further inquiry or an intentional exchange.

I call the specific kind of ongoing conversation that nurtures relationships connection or connecting conversations. Engaging in connecting conversations is central to sustaining a ministry for clergy and spiritual leaders. A connecting conversation can be exchanged between two people or a group. These conversations are curious about the person and the topic, about the context and the concerns, about the potential and the resistances. These conversations are intentional, not casual, about values such as fidelity, self-care and care for others, compassion, accountability, and respecting our shared humanity. These conversations have the potential to change a life.

In addition, prayer is a connecting conversation that nurtures a deep relationship and personal experience of God, of Jesus, and of the Holy Spirit. Such a conversation may mature into an enduring moment and an opening of a distinct direction or purpose for life. It can be a continual source of guidance. It will also ebb and flow throughout an individual's life. What is most important is that the conversation and the relationship continue as the individual grows and changes.

Yet this spiritual, prayerful conversation, by itself, is not enough to generate Connection within ourselves and with one another. Conversation with God and with one another fills the sails of human connection when three elements are present. First, we share our awareness of how our relationship with the Divine is growing with others, and then listen as they describe their relationship to God. Connections formed by shared awareness are often the strongest. Second, we recognize how our relationship with God shapes our intimate, private, and public relationships. God is not a remote bystander to our relationships. Our relationship with the Divine informs who we know ourselves to be as individuals and in community. And third, we acknowledge that God trusts and has compassion for us, which is the source of our ability to offer trust and compassion to our colleagues, close friends, family—and ourselves.

For example, the way one connects with trust and compassion in one's family life will change as marriages mature, children gain independence, and parents pass away. This is a connection fostered and frayed by daily exchanges, intimate moments, drying of tears, repairing teddy bears, and playful, spontaneous activities. At the same time, it is essential to recognize that a connection forged through trust and compassion is distinct when formed with colleagues who are asking similar questions, adapting to new conditions, learning new skills, and gaining new perspectives. In this case, to nurture the connection, those in the conversation must speak aloud their doubts and ask questions related to ministry or spiritual life. They must openly discuss the issues that matter in the town, or city, diocese, or nation.

Connection can be as simple as the joyful realization, "I feel this through my life with God, and you feel this, too!" Connection happens when someone shares, "My heart is breaking as the school shootings mount, and I want you to know how much I care," or "I would like us to work together to do something about it." Connection also occurs when we sit quietly together in sorrow because there is nothing to say in this deep grief.

How often do you have connecting conversations? How often do you share the multiple dimensions of your passion, or the heartbreaks that call out for action, one-on-one or in a group? While I do have these conversations from time to time with my close friends, I must confess that I rarely experience them at a clergy conference, or when meeting with my bishop, or with members of a congregation.

Connecting conversations need intention and preparation beforehand. Connection needs to be one with our minds and in our hearts for us to be open to seeing within the hearts of others and for them to see within ours. Revealing to others what we feel and what we honestly believe requires vulnerability. Surprisingly, we often discover that others feel and believe in ways that resonate within us even when we don't agree on everything.

What if the aim in a connecting conversation is to use words that feel right at a given moment? What if the aim is letting go of the precision requirement so that one open-ended thought draws inspiration from other thoughts? What if we value sharing spontaneously and become comfortable expressing an incomplete thought? What if we admit that we cannot articulate everything about a given experience? In a connecting conversation, we invite the Holy Spirit to move among us and inspire words within us.

A recent connecting conversation illustrates how stretching for precision and meaning is workable at some times but not at others. The participants prepared for this conversation by recalling an experience of compassion. One participant began describing her experience with wonder and great joyful energy. After a short while, though, she struggled for words. Then she started saying, "Oh, I don't know, I don't know." The energy and joy drained away. Her shoulders and head dropped. Another participant asked, "If you did know, then what would you say?" Her head popped up. She continued with enthusiasm, unhurried and untroubled by the need for precision. The words were hers just for today.

Ironically, sharing spontaneously and expressing incomplete thoughts requires preparation. Teachers and writers often say one cannot teach or write without knowing about the subject. Sharing spontaneously does not require rehearsing carefully written lines. Preparing involves reflecting on thoughts, ideas, and feelings, considering our own questions as well as those of our conversation partners. Sharing spontaneously flows from exploring the experience deeply, reflecting on it from different perspectives, and asking questions, so that spontaneous thoughts arise from a deep impression, forming mental images and word expressions.

Imagine a summer day with dispersed clouds that gather into towering cumulus formations. It is breathtaking. And those clouds were formed from the elements already present. Similarly, by focusing thoughts and feelings beforehand, the common focus has already begun to transform random ideas (the dispersed clouds) into a concentrated zone for making deeper connections among the members of the group during the conversation.

What is different about a connecting conversation? For example, when I leave a brainstorming session, I feel open, expansive, and creative. I feel an immense hopefulness. The future is now overflowing with possibilities. I do not worry about which possibility to choose because all possibilities are valuable. I do not need to choose any action at this point. A brainstorming session is primarily about generating ideas and harnessing the positive energy that comes with exploring numerous possibilities. A brainstorming session is about watching all the dispersed clouds.

In contrast, when I leave a connecting conversation, I feel grateful, I feel affirmed, I feel empowered to act on what I value, and I am encouraged to take even one step. I am a better person as a result of what I just learned about myself and the others present. I am ready to pursue my own goals and ready to help my colleagues pursue theirs. A connecting conversation is about feelings, the inner calm of affirmation, and the positive energy that comes from choosing an action that matters to me and is affirmed by the other participants.

The First Navigation Point: Growing Relationship with the Divine

I call this model Creating Connecting Conversations. And it is an exercise of reflective practice that all members of a congregation or participants in a group can follow. The invitation is to try the process and see what happens.

Creating Connecting Conversations

Visualize inviting five people to gather in person or online to have a conversation about God, relationships, and compassion.

- Where would you hold the conversation?
- What topic would you choose: God, relationships, or compassion?
- How would you focus on the topic?
- How would you help the other participants prepare for the conversation?
- What would you do after the conversation?

Visualize these steps so that you feel comfortable enough to extend the invitation.

EXAMPLE: When I picture the Connecting Conversation I would create, I see two couples, in addition to my husband and me. I would hold the conversation at my home from 1:00 to 2:30 on a Sunday afternoon to accommodate our group's family and work schedules. Light snacks accompanied by coffee and tea, with no alcohol. The focus is compassion. Participants prepare by identifying a story about compassion and arrive with the willingness to share why it is important to them. To help participants feel comfortable beforehand, I will invite each of them to offer an email introduction. After the conversation, I would follow up with an email or a voice call to thank each person for their contribution. I'd ask each if they would engage in another similar conversation. Would they recommend it to a friend? I would ask myself the same questions.

I caution against defaulting to a gathering pattern you already know, such as a social event or a dinner party. You are creating a *new* conversation practice. It is an iterative process that unfolds over time with each small gathering of people. Some groups might meet once. Other groups may continue through a designated number of meetings or until the group decides to conclude. Through your guidance and creation of intentional connecting conversations, each small gathering of people can discuss topics that are significant to the participants of the group.

A connecting conversation happens as an individual speaks about and shares their growing relationship with the Divine and then is also prepared to listen to the experiences of the others in the group. Doing so means that one must be open to listening to others who might share spiritual experiences they cannot fully describe. This approach may feel counterintuitive, since one is taught at seminary or through other ministry training to aim for precision in one's language and meaning. The traditional formation of soon-to-be-pastors as preachers and teachers encourages students to express their thoughts clearly and concisely for effective ministry.

The catalyst for connecting conversations is a reflection question that speaks to and addresses a value and a corresponding feeling. For me, the reflection question also encompasses a touch point greater than one's own being. Some call this Universal Being. I call the Ultimate One, greater than me, God. Intentional preparation that addresses common reflection questions connects us at our souls, the place God touches us, and where we touch God. We are comfortable sharing as clearly as we can today. Tomorrow we will have more to add to the conversation. We can be as thoughtful as we are able today. Tomorrow we can revise. This is what it looks and feels like when we talk in a connecting conversation about our flowing, growing life with God.

The navigation point for connecting conversations can be hard to locate because we rarely find ourselves in a conversation that models how to share our relationship with God with others. Spiritual direction, which is one-on-one or in a group, is one example of these intentional conversations. We usually talk about God in academic settings, sermons, and discussion groups. Rarely are we part of a conversation in which we describe a spiritual experience to others that is essential to who we are. We can initiate more groups for deeper conversations about belief, meaning, and daily living in Christ. The following model illuminates this navigation point and offers us confidence to enter into these kinds of conversations.

The Second Navigation Point: How God Shapes Relationships

Often on a sailboat, as the sails fill with wind, sailors rely on the lines (ropes attached to the sails themselves) to "shape" both the sails and the wind so that they work in tandem. In a comparable way, God shapes your intimate, private, and public relationships. God is integral to who you know yourself to be. Your relationships with others change over time. You change over time. Your relationship with God changes.

This ever-changing relationship is why I believe the prospect of undertaking connecting conversations feels risky to people. Sharing what is constantly evolving in your life, something that cannot be definitively pinned down, feels immature. Our accepted signs of maturity are consistency, self-regulation, and stability. Yet what if a sign of spiritual maturity is the willingness to investigate the depths and accept that there is always more to see?

When your life in ministry includes a trusted group of people with whom you engage in connecting conversations, there is an opportunity for those changes to be noticed and discussed. Intentional, focused conversations with this more intimate circle illuminate not only how you are changing but also how your conversation community members are evolving. As you speak, you see more clearly through your own eyes. When they speak with you, you see yourself more clearly through their eyes. And your comments to the participants offers your perspective so that they might see themselves more clearly.

Reflective Practice: Seeing the Shape of Your Relationships

Looking Deep

Do your intimate relationships have such depth that there is always more to see and learn?

How would you paint or draw a deep pond or an ocean? Would your perspective be from across the water or would it be looking down from above?

Looking Back
How has your spouse or partner changed in the last ten years? In the last five years? How have your spouse's depths influenced you?

Looking Forward
If you were to meet your future self in ten years, would you recognize yourself?

When Connecting Conversations Are Difficult

Connecting conversations are intended for anyone invited to participate. That may be a general invitation to all members of the parish or organization, with multiple conversation groups, or as the practice exercise describes, one group at a time by specific invitation.

However, since these intentional conversations are to share deeply held values and beliefs, choosing the appropriate invitation in your context is important. The expectations that congregation members can hold about clergy can make connecting conversations difficult. Clergy often face unspoken expectations: to maintain a gentle demeanor, dress modestly, smile consistently, appear free of personal problems because of their perceived closeness to God, remain constantly accessible, and be agreeable and malleable in their opinions.

The clergy person will inevitably disappoint at least one of those rigid expectations. Those unspoken expectations also might be about what a "generic clergy person" looks like. For example, while stereotypes about model white male clergy are changing, they are changing slowly. It is not unusual to hear parish members describe a clergy person as a white male in their thirties or forties, usually with a female spouse and kids. And it is not unusual for parish members to believe that this constellation of personal household—white, male, wife, and kids will—cause the parish to grow in attendance, solve stewardship giving, bring back the Sunday school, and relieve the volunteer decline.

Of course, parish members may not be aware of this unspoken expectation until a clergy person who is not white, male, and who does not fit the expectations is called to leadership at the parish. Only then do the unspoken expectations surface because parish members begin to feel that "things are not right," the person is "not a good fit," and everyone tastes bitter flavors of tension. Connecting conversations are not possible in these circumstances because too much is unsaid, and trust-building toward openness will not be possible.

The same is true when the expectation requires certain types of behavior from a clergy person and family members. As one example, I attended a dressy cocktail party at a parishioner's home. Another clergy person's spouse attended appropriately dressed for the occasion. The host approached and said, "I didn't know clergy wives could dress like that!" In the moment, we jokingly affirmed, "Of course she can," even as we recognized how deeply our host had insulted her and her husband.

Similarly, consider when a rector is deemed "not pastoral enough" simply for making decisions that certain members of the congregation find unpopular. The expected behavior in one area of the rector's role is transferred to administrative decisions to disparage the rector's competency. In this circumstance, trust does not exist, and it will be difficult to create connecting conversations.

I am not saying that the expectations of clergy make connecting conversation nearly impossible. And I am also not saying that all congregational members hold unspoken, unrealistic expectations of clergy leaders. I am saying that as a clergy leader initiating a connecting conversation, choosing your conversation partners requires wisdom. Set up conversational safety for yourself. Choose participants wisely. Be explicit about the process, the norms, confidentiality, and the questions to be answered. Experience will teach you what to look for. After several conversations, you can expand the process beyond your original conversation partners and start other connecting conversation groups.

Also, be confident that a connecting conversation brings inner change. Relationships within this group will usually grow deeper than your relationships with other members of your congregation. If you have ever been a mentor or part of an Education for Ministry (EfM) group, then you likely experienced how members of that learning community have a deep understanding of one another. Yet, as a leader in most of your public functions, it is crucial to remember that you are expected to respond to all members evenly.

Some try to handle this by remaining the same person in public and stifling any outward signs of inner change: happy and jolly on the surface, and no one's expectations are upset. Yet, you are living in two places. Realize that you will need to recognize when you are isolating your growing spiritual and personal maturity.

A compassionate and skilled spiritual director, as well as your intentional conversation community, can offer wisdom on how to let the important people in your public life know how you are changing. Who, how, and when are specific to your situation. For example, let's say you must make a major decision as a leader, and you know the changes you have experienced in your spiritual life will impact the decision. Formulating your own pivotal views about the decision will be helpful, but it will be important to share those views with those who will carry out the decision, as well as those impacted by it.

Final Navigation Point: Trust and Compassion

The third and final navigation point of connecting conversations is the trust you place in colleagues and the compassion you have for yourself.

> When you meet a new colleague, do you say any of the following to yourself?
>
> - "I trust everyone until they show me otherwise."
> - "I wade into the pool slowly and cautiously."
> - "I do not trust anyone until I know them well enough."

Do you recognize any of these approaches as yours? Each approach is one of three points on the general spectrum of trust. We can begin with complete, unbounded trust. This first type of trust is innocent and childlike. For example, this type of trust bears inner messages such as "nothing can happen to me," or "I will only react when it hurts," or "the other person will take care not to hurt me." The only person who can provide circumstances that guard against you being hurt, taken advantage of, or misunderstood is you.

The second type of trust is to wait and see and measure the outcome. This trust takes in information about the other person, shares information about yourself, and gently tests for follow-through, consistency, and reliability. Mutual trust builds through what you experience about the other person and what they experience about you. The give and take form the relationship at a moderate pace.

This third point on the general spectrum of trust is complete distrust until safety is proven to be a reliable expectation. You are gathering information about your colleague while carefully titrating the information you share about yourself. With this slow drip, the experience of the relationship builds slowly to the level of your comfort before you are ready to enter with any self-disclosure.

Why is it important to be aware of your approach to trust? Because your new colleague or conversation partner will sense your philosophy of trust. At the beginning of my ministry, for example, one conversation I had with a colleague from another denomination fell into the category of open sharing, asking questions, and engaging in meaningful dialogue. We met for lunch. I assumed part of the purpose of the lunch was to get to know one another. So, I chatted, asking her questions and letting her get to know me. At the end of the lunch, she remarked how uncomfortable she felt and asked if I was uncomfortable too. When I replied "No," her response was that she was also a therapist and not accustomed to sharing so much about herself. My pace of information sharing exceeded her accustomed pace. To her, the conversation felt like an instant relationship. I wish I had known she was a therapist, too, or that she had mentioned it at some point.

Also, note that any of these approaches can prove to be either an asset or a liability. Employing each approach requires you to set a boundary for your colleague to prove themselves. You may have also unwittingly put up a shield. Most likely, the approach depends on the person, their role in your life, and spans multiple points on the relational spectrum. But there is another approach you can use.

> When you meet a new colleague, do you say any of the following to yourself?
>
> - What do I want my conversation partner to observe in me?
> - How might my conversation partner feel as we talk together?
> - What do I value in myself that I bring to this conversation?

In other words, you can decide ahead of time how you will demonstrate the values that nurture trust, consistency, honesty, openness, and humility. An effective spiritual leader models these values on a daily basis.

Imagine for a moment a leader chairing a meeting for the first time. Participants are getting to know one another. More importantly, they are getting to know the leader by observing how she conducts the meeting and how she behaves. A leader who has a clear grasp of her values plans how to model them while chairing the committee. She could do the following:

- Scheduling and then adhering to meeting dates for consistency
- Developing a clear agenda prior to the meeting for open communication
- During the meeting, inviting different voices and balancing different opinions for openness
- During and after the meeting, demonstrating clarity as well as care for all members of the group
- After the meeting, refusing to comment about one member of the committee to another to maintain confidentiality and build trust

A spiritual leader also demonstrates openness and humility by collaborating with the congregational leadership, typically the elected leaders of a vestry or other governing body, to articulate the possibilities, challenges, and vision for the congregation. This collaboration assumes the leader can clearly articulate a vision rooted in the congregation's specific theological commitments and its unique community calling. The spiritual leader must listen for a shared vision, guide communication and discussion, move to actionable items, and continue learning along the way.

This approach is a tall order. And it is very different than beginning with the usual hierarchical method that concludes with "the vestry voted on the strategic plan." Instead, collaboration becomes the framework for all discussions. The hierarchical method might be the final step if the debate over moving forward goes on indefinitely. But that final step doesn't happen until leadership makes the clearly communicated decision to move forward with a vote. In the meantime, all leaders of the congregation continue to act with openness and humility.

The tools provided below this collaborative approach enable the leader to model not only trustworthiness but also to be recognized as trustworthy by colleagues. Equally important, those colleagues observe norms that can guide their own behavior.

Tools of Trust

Take an inventory of when and how you create your meeting agendas, and notice when and how a leader models consistency, clear communication, and caring.

1. Draw a line down the center of a page. At the top of one column, mark Self. At the top of the other column, mark Others, meaning a group of other leaders such as the vestry, board, or group of directors.
2. Review your meetings from the past month, making notes about how trustworthiness was modeled in each column.
3. Note what you would like to change about your meeting leadership.
4. Note what skills and qualities you admired in the "Other" list, and what you would like to incorporate into your own leadership approach.

Overlooked No More: Self-Compassion

Compassion connects. Remember my observation that upon meeting a new colleague, that person will sense your stance on trust? That same colleague will also sense the degree of compassion you have for yourself. And when they sense you possess self-compassion, they trust you will show that same compassion for them. It is therefore a question to ask yourself: Are you creating safety for them and for you?

Recalling the two stories at the beginning of this chapter, do you think a connecting conversation is likely to occur between the newly arrived rector and the senior colleague? The senior colleague demonstrates little interest in the personal circumstances of the new rector or in setting professional boundaries. He shows little compassion toward understanding her and himself. Instead, he responds with an overworn phrase, "rectors never get a day off," challenging the new rector's balance of ministry. Her first self-disclosure is met with criticism and a view that ministry is a grind. The two criteria for a connecting conversation, trust and compassion, are not present. My guess is that the tone of this hypothetical lunch meeting will be friendly, consist mostly of small talk, and include expert, top-down advice.

An often overlooked form of compassion for clergy and spiritual leaders is self-compassion. Self-compassion is a popular topic now. It differs from self-care, which describes a discipline to claim time for yourself in a profession and vocation where the prevailing role of most in the organization is that of a caregiver.

An understanding of self-compassion, on the other hand, begins with neuroscience. The science tells us that, by nature, human beings compare one situation with another, one scenario with another, as a means of survival. I see a tiger. Is it going to eat me? How dangerous is this situation? Do I need to keep walking? Run? Hide? Play dead?

Fortunately, most often our own lives do not require us to compare one situation over another based on survival stakes. But we do compare ourselves against other people, don't we? If we do not meet a cultural norm such as being fit enough, humble enough, or tall enough, such comparisons can flood our minds with negative self-talk. While we learn this behavior from parents, coaches, teachers, or other significant adults during our formative years, other negative self-talk issues stem from a need to demonstrate that our situation is better than others. "At least my illness, or marriage problem, or difficult coworker is not as bad as my friend who has . . ." I often hear this observation as a priest. This tendency is known as upward self-comparison. Someone is always worse off than we are, so we feel better. We are also grateful that we are not dealing with the more difficult problem our friend is experiencing.

Alternatively, we might put ourselves down in comparison to others. This tendency is known as downward self-comparison. Recall a time when you have said or heard a phrase such as, "I am terrible at math," or "I can't administrate myself out of a paper bag," or "I am the most disorganized person around." When someone remarks on their perceived personal flaws before anyone else does, they are putting up a personal protective shield.

Kristin Neff is a significant researcher and writer in the field of neuroscience. She defines three core components of practicing self-compassion: self-kindness, recognition of common humanity, and mindfulness.[2] According to Neff, because we create our own mindset, we can allow this negative self-talk to narrate our life story. Or we can apply self-kindness, recognize our shared humanity, and practice mindfulness. In her writings and talks, Neff provides exercises that build one's capacity to maintain a positive self-view and narrative for one's life.

One exercise is the Self-Compassion Break.[3] This exercise and dozens of others are found in the Mindful Self-Compassion program, which Neff developed, and in her book, cowritten with Christopher Germer, PhD.

The Self-Compassion Break can be done at any time when you feel you need a pause and your inner resources need refreshment. I like to imagine the sound of clear flowing water. The following words from Neff summarize the process.

Choose a situation that is moderate, such as a 5 on a scale of 1 to 10. At the beginning of practicing self-compassion breaks, starting with the most intense situations, the roughest waters, is not advised. Allow yourself to recall the situation. Notice what you are feeling in your body. Where do you feel the sensations

2. Kristin Neff, *Fierce Self Compassion: How to Harness Kindness to Speak Up, Claim Your Power, and Thrive* (Harper Perennial, 2021).

3. Kristin Neff, *The Mindful Self-Compassion Workbook, A Proven Way to Accept Yourself, Build Inner Strength, and Thrive* (The Guilford Press, 2021), 34-35.

most? Maybe your gut, your chest, your head, another place. Locate the sensations of this moment. Then, say to yourself, "This really hurts," or "I am really hurting," or This is suffering." The exact language is not a formula. Find words that work for you. The exercise at this point is to use the wisdom of your body to assist you in feeling the discomfort and pain, and then recognize that suffering is present. This is mindfulness to be aware of what you are experiencing, in this case, to feel what you are feeling, in the moment.

Next, expand the awareness of your suffering to all of life. Calmly, you might say, "Suffering is part of life," or "Struggling feels like this to me and others." Your words connect you to your common humanity.

Finally, offer yourself the tender self-compassion of love and friendliness. Place your hands on a part of your body that feels soothing, such as your heart or belly. The words to yourself are accepting, such as "May I accept myself as I am now, today," or "May I be understanding and patient with myself," or "May I be kind to myself." Find words for yourself that are words you would speak to a good friend. Speaking to yourself with care, calmness, understanding, and being a good friend to yourself is self-kindness.

Allow a few moments to appreciate your self-compassion break before returning to the rest of your day.[4]

4. Ibid., 34–35.

This Self-Compassion Break guides participants through the three aforementioned key elements of self-compassion: mindfulness, common humanity, and self-kindness. The order and focus provided in the exercise guide the participant through noticing and naming individual "dis-ease," noticing and naming the dis-ease of all human beings, and noticing and naming the innate tenderness and care we have within ourselves. I encourage you to turn to Neff's book or the workbook to fully engage with the exercise and repeat it whenever you need it.

Practicing self-compassion enhances the wholeness we experience within ourselves and exponentially increases the compassion we share with others out into the world.

Self-compassion connects. Practices for self-compassion in everyday life are accessible to fit into the time you have or the time you choose to create. Here are a few suggestions to engage the foundational elements of self-kindness, common humanity, and mindfulness.

Other Resources for Reflective Practices: Self-Compassion

Self-Kindness

Ask yourself at least three times a day, "Would I respond to my friend the way I just responded to myself?"

Loving Kindness Meditations

Sharon Salzberg is a pioneer of mindfulness education. One of her books is *Open to Life,* an at-home retreat featuring short chapters on various meditation practices. Her Loving Kindness meditation is one of them. The book is available in audio form so that participants can listen to the text as a guided meditation.[5]

Mindfulness

Another pioneer in mindfulness education is Jon Kabat-Zinn. He defines mindfulness as the awareness that arises through paying attention in a particular way, on purpose, in the present moment, non-judgmentally. Zinn is a medical researcher and author of many books, including *Full Catastrophe Living: Using the Wisdom of Your Body and Mind to Face Stress, Pain, and Illness.*[6] FCL, as it is known, is the foundation of the Mindfulness-Based Stress Reduction (MBSR) program he developed as an intervention for patients with chronic conditions. Developed over forty years ago, MBSR is now an experimentally validated intervention taught worldwide. The foundational elements of meditation, the origins of stress, appreciation of common humanity, and experiential learning facilitated through dialogue within each

---

5. Sharon Salzberg, *Open to Life: Learning to Love Yourself and the World* (MacMillan Audio, 2021).

6. Jon Kabat-Zinn, *Full Catastrophe Living: Using the Wisdom of Your Body and Mind to Face Stress, Pain, and Illness* (Bantam, 1990).

cohort are taught over eight weeks. One of the centers for enrolling in an MBSR class is the School of Public Health at Brown University: https://www.mindfulness.sph.brown.edu.

Common Humanity

Self-compassion can also mean discovering your strengths and gifts. Ask yourself, "What strength did I consistently use this past week?" Your identity is what you do well, what comes naturally to you, and what you enjoy doing. So asking yourself this question will increase your self-understanding and self-awareness. You come to know yourself more fully.

Tools like the Clifton StrengthsFinder[7] and VIA Character Strengths[8] are accessible online. Consider what strengths you require in others. Could the other spiritual leaders in your congregation or organization partner with you to share your strengths for the benefit of the congregation?

A clergy leader may be strong at developing the congregation's vision. This strength complements another congregation leader who can follow up, set priorities, and act to move the project forward. Or a congregational leader may excel at decisions that require extensive deliberation, careful attention to detail, and thoughtful anticipation of obstacles.

---

7. https://www.gallup.com/topic/cliftonstrengths.aspx
8. https://viacharacter.org

A partnership with another congregational leader who is strong in communication is needed to craft the big picture presentation for the congregation. All leaders require partners. And connecting your strengths with those of the other leaders leverages the entire team's strengths for the benefit of the congregation or organization. And the results are only a portion of this connection. When offering strengths, each person experiences a deep connection within themselves and with others at all levels of the project.

Centering Prayer and Contemplation

One path within Christianity to our inner heart with God is Centering Prayer. It resembles mindfulness in its deep awareness of the present moment and its ability to expand awareness. The practice allows one to face the realities of each day. It differs from mindfulness in a significant way, though: It is not an attention-focusing activity, but rather a practice of letting go. By letting go of thoughts to which you cling for identity, you open yourself to experiencing God's presence at the center of your God-created being. Traditionally, Centering Prayer is practiced twice a day.

> The first step of the basic Centering Prayer Practice is choosing a sacred word. One word is best. Classic examples are *Jesus*, *Spirit*, *love*, and *hope*.

Set a timer for ten minutes. Find a comfortable seat that allows your feet to touch the floor and your back to remain straight and supported.

Start your timer. Close your eyes.

After a couple of deep, relaxing breaths, imagine your thoughts are loaded onto a ship that is sailing away from the harbor. Each time a thought comes into your head, return to your sacred word to let go of yourself and remain open to God. Return to your sacred word as many times as is needed. (You will experience many, *many* thoughts. That is normal. When those thoughts sweep in, gently return to the sacred word.)

Strong emotions may arise, which is a normal response. Allow them to be unless you become flooded with them. Should that occur, open your eyes and conclude your Centering Prayer "sit" (as it is known) for this day. When you are ready, reflect on those feelings. Try Centering Prayer again.

Over time, increase the duration of your "sit" to twenty minutes. The location of your "sit" can be anywhere—on the beach, alone, or with a Centering Prayer Group. Centering Prayer is not a practice to attempt while driving or engaging in activities that require your full attention.

Thomas Keating, a Trappist priest, revived the ancient practice of Christian contemplation and developed the practice of Centering Prayer.

He wrote numerous books, including *Open Mind, Open Heart* (Continuum, 2006). He also founded Contemplative Outreach (https://www.contemplativeoutreach.org), a community for the practice of Centering Prayer. The members of Contemplative Outreach offer international, national, and regional resources for everyone, the curious, the new practitioner, and the longtime contemplative.

Summary

Connection is our deepening awareness of God, ourselves, and one another. While we can run aground on a sandbar of "isn't it awful" conversations, we can also discover the navigation points of connecting conversations. Creating connecting conversations fills our sails with the wind of the Holy Spirit and brings us closer both to God and others. By shaping our sails in our intimate and public relationships, we grow in self-awareness. We will navigate a journey of connection toward trust and self-compassion, being alert not to sail past the point of trust and underestimate the importance of the emerging navigation point of self-compassion. Connection is the first leg of our leadership journey. Connection is the discovery that we do not travel alone. We travel with dynamic new ministry partners.

CHAPTER 2
Clarity and Momentum

Watch the Gap between the Dock and the Boat

The newly ordained curate arrived at his office on a dazzling September morning, ready to embrace all that parish ministry could be. After all, for four years as an active member of his local parish, he had met with a discernment group about his call. The Commission on Ministry process took the usual two years, after which he dove into theological studies, earning the required three-year Master of Divinity degree. The ordination the previous Saturday was exuberant, followed on Sunday by the celebration of his first Eucharist. For the past ten years, he had been moving toward this moment.

As requested, he stopped by the rector's office. Looking up, the rector waved him in. What followed was a speech about making sure the curate was ready for ministry. The curate was to learn from the altar guild first. Next, he would spend three weeks with the church musician, who would explain how musical practices were carried out in this parish. Then it was on to the Tuesday morning Bible study for the seniors, followed by working as a food server at the Thursday soup kitchen. Oh, and because the rector was taking a two-week vacation in January, the curate would cover the preaching, celebrating, and pastoral care during that time.

The curate asked questions about meeting members of the congregation through pastoral visits, preaching, celebrating the Eucharist, and teaching. "All in due time," replied the rector. Of course, the weekday Eucharist needed a celebrant who included a homily. The curate would also "see how things are done" during a confirmation class taught by the rector.

What had not been discussed was the curate's, the rector's, and their bishop's concept of a first-year curate position. Expectations were not discussed. No job description was provided. It seemed to the curate that the tasks associated with this position were whatever and however they formed in a person's mind. As months passed, due to this utter lack of clarity about the position and its responsibilities, the curate, the rector, and, finally, their bishop were all profoundly disappointed. The dynamics of their relationship felt like sandpaper. Trust was low.

The vague, distant, and unsuccessful relationship the rector launched with the curate is only one aspect of this story. The most important aspect involves the gap. By that, I mean the gap in expectations. The newly ordained priest made the reasonable assumption that he would be an integral part of the parish's ministry from his first day on the job. Conversely, the rector held the traditional assumption that he controlled the curate's formation and involvement in the parish ministry. And the bishop? The bishop could make many assumptions, among them that this experienced priest would know exactly how to incorporate the curate into the life of the parish.

I have heard variations on this story repeatedly. The scenario I hear second most often is that of the curate who has had enough of trying to collaborate with a rector and goes to the bishop. The bishop will reassign the new priest sometime in the next year. And guess what? Shortly after, that same rector receives a new curate.

I have not encountered a rector-curate scenario in which conversations are used to address the gap in expectations. Neither have I heard of a scenario in which a bishop provides rectors with a template of activities and ministry assignments that promise to give the newly ordained priest appropriate hands-on experience.

What does a new clergy person learn when a lack of clarity and a gap in expectations define the first years of ministry? Because they have been forced to navigate the gap, they have developed skepticism and distrust of other clergy, including the bishop.

Rectors fall victim to navigating the gap too. In the gap, a rector does not reflect on a model for formation in a curacy, does not develop a collaborative approach for identifying what a curate needs to learn, and does not compose a clear, detailed job description. What the rector learns is that his or her best efforts do not "work."

A bishop navigates the gap by attempting to understand the viewpoints of both the rector and the curate, yet fails to consider what learning model might be built based on the criteria set by the bishop and mutual understanding among all involved.

A conscientious boat captain will remind passengers when boarding and exiting the boat to watch the gap between the dock and the boat deck. Water and wind conditions may shift this gap as passengers cross it. Watch the gap reminders are helpful in other areas of parish life. Church organizations operate along relationship lines established by clergy and members, spiritual leaders and active members, liturgies and all members, staff and the priest, and the priest and the vestry. Each of those relationships also includes gaps.

Clarity: The Meeting Point

What is *clarity* in ministry practice relationships?

Clarity is the point where expectations turn into a shared and mutually agreed-upon understanding of what the issue is and the steps to address it. In the story above, each spiritual leader, curate, rector, and bishop, has a different expectation about the curate's job. Along with each different expectation goes a different set of questions. The curate expects to be a full part of every ministry. His question is: "How do I integrate myself into the life of the parish?" He is looking to his supervisor, the rector, for guidance on where to begin and how to prioritize the process.

The rector, on the other hand, expects help. He is asking, "How can I train this new priest to be my assistant so that he understands how this parish works and how he can be most helpful?" The rector answers that question by introducing the curate to what the rector considers key constituencies in the parish. The bishop expects a priest who will be a full member of the diocese. He is asking, "How will this new priest be formed in a healthy priestly identity?" The bishop answers this question by placing the new priest with an experienced priest.

The first step on the journey toward clarity is for each person to state a question, problem, or issue. The gap scenario above, written from the curate's point of view, illustrates the new priest's expectations, implied questions, and the impact of disappointment. The work of defining, shaping, and refining that leads to clarity begins with each individual involved identifying their specific expectations, questions, and issues.

A leader tends to look in a particular direction with a fixed endpoint. This makes it tempting to suggest that there is an answer to be named, and it is the desired strategic result. However, fully identifying the issue means identifying the various perspectives involved. Looking for an answer from only the curate's perspective will not create a meeting point with the rector and the bishop. Their expectations are completely different.

The second step to clarity is to share all perspectives to *identify* the issue common to all three participants in this scenario. The issue in our scenario is not the content of the curate's job description. It is much more complex. The issue is the gap in expectations among all three people. The curate wants to know how he will be part of the parish. The rector wants to know how the curate will provide meaningful assistance, and the bishop wants the new priest to learn healthy habits for the practice of ministry and for the rector to have help with his ministry. Addressing the expectations gap requires each individual to adapt in order to help bridge that divide.

For the curate, rector, and bishop, clarity invites these reflective questions: What do I believe the question to be? How do I describe what I think the job of the curate is? How do I define the problem or adaptation? Where do I stand emotionally and spiritually? What are my strengths? Where do I need help? When the issue is addressed among the three participants, what communication is needed for the congregation, diocese, and colleagues?

Let us focus on the word *communicate* for a moment. In ministry practice, whether you realize it or not, your organization judges you as a leader by how you navigate a challenge or issue and what the result looks like. Discovering how to connect with yourself emotionally, spiritually, and vocationally (i.e., self-awareness) is a valuable skill for defining and refining clarity-related questions.

For example, to refine how the conversation to address the issue might take shape in advance, the curate, rector, and bishop could each reflect on these questions: what if I have come to recognize that my initial description of the expectation, question, or issue does not describe what I really want to say? To further identify the real issue, I must ask additional questions. Moreover, I invariably require help framing the question from a trusted colleague, mentor, or coach. And then there is the fact that other dynamics color what words I use to describe an issue. History, context, a need to feel safe, uncertainty, emotions, and hoped-for outcomes are examples of filters that can color initial attempts to state the issue. Recognizing or removing those filters is crucial to the process, as is committing to making "I" statements, because inevitably we all have blind spots.

In the basic flow of the process, each person individually reflects on these questions. The curate engages his own reflection following the pattern of the questions. The rector also reflects on the pattern. The bishop also engages in this process.

Through this reflective process, each person finds different ways to state the issue, share insights, and discover possible solutions.

Given the practical realities of ministry, it is hard for me to imagine, although not impossible, a conversation among the bishop, rector, and curate. More likely, the curate and the rector will meet to define the issue. It can be helpful for each person to write down the definition and possible action steps in advance to share with the other person. With preparation, the rector and the curate identify goals, strengths, and areas for learning that come together to create and plan how they will offer ministry together in that parish. This may seem like an overly involved first-time conversation, but the initial deliberate effort creates clarity that will save significant time later.

- Often, we do not sort out all these questions and come to the heart of an issue on our own. A mentor, which we will learn more about in chapter 5, can direct our focus toward clarity by asking such powerful questions as: "What is the most important of the five ideas we identified?"
- "Which is the idea that you wish to work on today?"
- "Which idea are you resisting and why?"

The mentor's role is to identify and state what are inevitably multiple issues, repeat them, and reframe them until the leader declares, "Yes, that is the most important issue!"

As part of my clarity process, here are questions I ask myself that are variations of those asked by mentors:

- "What is the most important thing for me to learn in this upcoming conversation?"
- "What is the most important thing for me to describe to my conversation partner?"
- "What is the most important alternative that I want to offer to my conversation partner?"

To continue to hear voices of clarity beyond these initial reflections, maintaining a long-term relationship with a mentor is beneficial. A mentor can broaden the view by asking more questions. "Have you stumbled over a similar issue? How did you work on it then, and how do you want to work on it now?" A mentor who knows you not only has a nuanced view of you as a person and as a spiritual leader but also brings years of ministry experience to their mentoring role. Such a mentor is like a seasoned sailor who understands that the practice of ministry is ever changing and requires adjusting the metaphorical sails to the dynamics of the conditions. She or he is the traveling companion who can not only navigate but also help you observe and reflect on what you have learned in the past that could be helpful now, what did not work well in the past, and what has proved effective.

For example, as a mentor, when I guide reflective work, I also invite the individual to go deeper by exploring what this new clarity reveals, where are the emotionally tender places, what spiritual insights arise, and to look deeply into waters we rarely disturb.

Another possibility for continuing conversations for clarity is reflection with a single trusted partner. The connection is already solid; with this person's vulnerability, self-revelation, doubt, and deeper discovery, it feels comfortable.

During this kind of intentional conversation, the individual seeks clarity and describes the process of reflection offered above. Next, the individual also shares the clarity that they realized through the process of individual reflection. Since a solid foundation of trust is present in the dialogue, the trusted partner can identify filters or biases that the person reflecting may not see. The conversation may entail unwinding various issues, reframing, and restating.

One result of this process is to become accustomed to the tender places. This can be an important rehearsal for the actual conversation between the curate and the rector when individuals are not in mutual agreement. Then, those tender places are less likely to be a trigger. In the actual conversation, we may reach a meeting place of agreement *and* disagreement. Inner clarity supports living with both.

Those tender places also reveal the emotional gap between a change event and the adjustments needed to fully embrace it. During major life changes, people often lose clarity. They may mistake the moment of change—the change event—for the transition that follows, when both emotional and physical shifts start to unfold.

A change event is a point in time when a familiar way of living ends, and another is about to begin. For example, it can be a momentous life event, such as baptism, graduation, ordination, professional certification, relocation to a new home or setting, marriage, childbirth, an unexpected change in income, illness, death, and bereavement. These are complex and highly emotional events. A change event does not necessarily mean that those experiencing the change have incorporated its consequences into their lives. The change becomes real and recognized only after the subsequent transition period, during which personal, spiritual, emotional, logistical, community, and relational shifts occur to create a different way of life. Ministry practice involves shepherding one's people through the change event and the transition period.

When we believe that a change event fully accomplishes the change, we expect the group or individual we are leading to act from a newly formed dimension of identity. Then we prematurely ask ourselves, "Why are things not going as planned?" "Why is the anxiety out of control?" "What happened to these reasonable, rational people who accepted this change?"

What is happening is that the change event moves into the next transition stage, rearranging, refining, and adding new knowledge within the group or the individual. Those within our stewardship as leaders and those within our care as spiritual leaders are experiencing transition as a new way of being themselves, a new identity.

Guiding people through the transition stage reveals greater clarity for the whole community or organization. Throughout the transition, they continue to adjust in both large and small ways. The community needs time in the transition stage to arrive at the change. As leaders in ministry practice, if we mistake the change event for arriving at the change, we disregard the potential of the transition and leave people behind.

For the curate, clarity can be lost as he adjusts emotionally, spiritually, and vocationally to a series of changing events from graduation to arriving at his first job. His life is in the transition stage, including figuring out what his job really is now that there is a gap in expectations. It would be a normal reaction that a gap in expectations also adds to the unsettled state of transition. Awareness of those tender places as normal can help him prepare for the conversation about that gap.

Hearing from voices within your ministry context is also key to clarity. Peer learning groups composed of colleagues at a similar stage in ministry practice offer perspectives that you cannot see on your own. Peers may also notice a trait or emotional trigger of which you are unaware. Moreover, a peer learning group, which we learn more about in chapter 5, understands your context, parish culture, history, and significant individuals within the parish.

Adding to the benefits of a peer learning community is engaging in conversation with trusted, experienced clergy. I believe that an experienced clergy person, trained as a mentor to facilitate a peer group, creates the possibility for developing rich, full, and complex perspectives among the members of the peer group. A clergy person with lifelong experience can foresee what might lie ahead farther down the leadership road because they have already traveled it. Leadership and ministerial dynamics appear and feel different from the vantage point of experience. Or this perspective could also reveal that you have based your understanding of an issue on a faulty assumption.

Reflect on the Perspectives in The Gap

Reread "the gap" scenario at the beginning of this chapter.

- How would you write the questions from the curate's perspective?
- How would you write the scenario from the rector's point of view?
- How would you write the scenario from the bishop's point of view?

This is a free writing exercise. Open a notebook or sit down at your laptop and write from the three perspectives referenced above. Spend ten minutes writing from each point of view. You can complete all three points of view at one time or take one at a time.

Momentum: Moving Parts Working Together

Do you feel it? The movement of Spirit is like the wind beginning to fill your leadership sail. Working toward clarity is not an end in itself. Clarity generates *momentum*. The Holy Spirit is at work in this sacred collaborative learning process. You are moving forward.

Gaining clarity is deliberate and intentional. If you are a curate working toward clarity, you likely now have a deeper understanding of yourself. You can articulate what you need and want for ministry and have shaped these ideas with the awareness that two others—the rector and the bishop—are part of the conversation. You recognize that agreement on the issue is essential and that multiple action steps may be proposed to address it.

You know your outer and inner clarity. You know you can be both in agreement and in disagreement. You may not receive everything you wish to from the conversation with the other partners in the situation. Then, there will be new steps to take with others—exploring different places and connecting with people who can help you gain the experience you seek. In other words, instead of reaching a *stopping* point in the conversation, you arrive at a *starting* point filled with possibilities and options.

The first movements need not occur quickly. After all, a light breeze allows a boat to glide forward. One "gentle" question to generate momentum is "How would you like to work on this issue?" In the peer group, as each member contributes, the number of possibilities for moving forward increases. Select one, two, or three ideas to try as potential "navigation points." Remember, the boat will be moving not in a random direction, but on a course you have carefully considered. Friction or resistance to moving forward is inevitable. These will affect momentum. And so will the energy generated from your well-informed idea and the wind of the Holy Spirit blowing into your sail. The power of the wind, sails, boat, rudder, and a skilled crew work together toward the way forward.

Just like a boat gliding through the water, momentum is freeing. Now I'm no longer stuck in my own head, bumping up against my own perspective and answers. In that condition, I am quite confident that everyone else is uninformed and unfair. Not a good condition to continually ask questions. But with clarity and trust, now the questions can flow. I can look around. I can appreciate the changing wind on my face, knowing with each puff I will need to adjust a sail, or a line, or the rudder. And my overall course will not change. Free to move, free to adjust, free to move forward.

Too often, we can believe that ministry practice is about being stuck, waiting for some outside force to act on us and change the conditions. The bishop retires. The antagonist leaves the parish. The matriarch moves out of town to be closer to her family. We change parishes. Usually, we find out that those same external conditions exist in other places.

Ministry practice is about finding momentum. The pieces fit together to move. In parishes, this might be a sizable project, such as starting a community farmer's market in a local food desert. In this example, there are many pieces to fit together, many people to bring together, likely several competing needs to address, logistical challenges, and regulatory requirements. The entry ramp may be long. Finding the momentum in each connecting piece moves the project over the longest of entry ramps.

The pieces may be in less complex projects like weeding the garden beds, knitting prayer shawls, or the monthly men's group. The momentum depends on the leader's connection with others, coming to clarity, knowing the components, and putting them together so that a program takes shape and keeps going.

The speed of our momentum will vary, depending on the complexities of changing people, relationships, expectations, and circumstances. The key for those in ministry is to recognize their resources and put the pieces together so they can move forward together. Mentors and peer groups are resources I described above. Other trusted supports, such as spiritual directors and therapists, can also be valuable resources for the tender, vulnerable, and deeper exploration.

We all have the capability for reflection. As human beings, we share the capacity for wonder, creativity, and the ability to imagine possible outcomes. As friends of Jesus, we have the capability to envision a world shaped by the principles He lived. In a faith tradition that places humanity in relationship to the Divine being, we all have the capacity to see the Divine as greater than our individual selves and yet shared among all beings. While we have the capacity, we may need to develop the capability to use and grow our capacity. We tap into and grow our capacity through intentional reflection.

Reflect on the Foundational Questions of the Gap

Let's go back to "the gap" scenario. The situation can happen that the curate schedules a meeting with the rector to discuss the job description. This would be a reasonable approach when the individual is in a new position. And, let's assume that the curate did not have the benefit of the reflective process above. This can also be a typical approach. Instead, his questions are spontaneous and powered by emotion. Usually, the consequences of this type of meeting do not result in mutual understanding and clarity.

If you were in his position, how would you strengthen your ability to build momentum by taking time before the meeting to clarify what to ask? What might you do differently?

For example:

- What are your expectations of yourself to do your job well?
- Can you be curious about the rector's expectations about what a job well done looks like?
- You cannot ask what you do not know. Can you be curious about what you do not know? How would you like the rector to support your learning?
- Can you describe what you would like to learn, knowing the rector is likely to add to your list?
- Reflect on how your own questions are impacting you and your ministry.

With the list of your questions, write a sixty-second summary of the questions as an invitation to the rector for a conversation. Believe it or not, sixty seconds is about as long as one person can maintain attention when they know the invitation is to a conversation about addressing gaps, potential conflicts, and going deeper. You will write down more questions than can fit in the sixty-second time limit. Be specific. You can address the "extra" questions during a future conversation. In this first conversation, you are laying the foundation for a learning relationship.

I recommend that you try the above exercise before meeting with the rector. In the following example, I do not want to shape or direct how you would reflect to prepare for the conversation. Here is one way a sixty-second summary might go:

"I would like to start a conversation with you about the questions I have. I have my own expectations about a job well done that I would like you to consider, and I would appreciate hearing your expectations as well. I have a feeling (instinct, thought, idea—whatever word sounds right to you) that we overlap and, in some places, don't overlap. I am curious and enthusiastic about learning as much as I can, and at the same time, I cannot ask questions about things I do not know. I am wondering if you can support me as I learn, and what that would look like? Would you be interested in discussing these questions with me?"

In this hypothetical example, the conversation's purpose is clearly stated in the first sentence. Your conversation partner, this time the rector, now has a good idea of what is coming.

"I" language conveys that what you are saying is your point of view, for which you do not need to be apologetic or hesitant. You are also clearly asking for the rector's point of view.

Finally, you are inviting the rector into a future conversation. The conversation *now* launches future conversations. It is likely that this initial conversation will need to be refined in some areas and expanded in others. This beginning conversation can set the tone.

Reading this summary aloud takes less than sixty seconds.

It might unfold that the conversation begins immediately. It might unfold that a time is scheduled. Initially, it's a good idea to prepare invitations and questions for each conversation. Reflecting ahead of time with the resources you create, such as peers and mentors, can help you identify the issue so that the urge to stay comfortably in the questions does not take over. Mutually agreeing on the issue means the conversation is going somewhere. It might be small, and yet a direction is chosen. An action will be taken. Something is going to happen. Momentum will start.

Ministry practice is about finding momentum. Rather than being stuck and still, momentum is a flow of movement along the chosen direction. Friction and resistance are inherent to the dynamics of adaptation. As the moving wind fills the sails, you can begin to see and feel the momentum. Maintaining the movement, tending to it, and adjusting to the dynamics of changing conditions around it steer us toward the next chapter on reflective practice.

CHAPTER 3
Reflective Practice

I do not call you servants any longer, because the servant does not know what the master is doing; but I have called you friends, because I have made known to you everything that I have heard from my Father.

—John 15:15

Two newly certified accountants launched their own practices. The first accountant signed up clients quickly. He worked efficiently and with accuracy. He maintained the ethics of the field and a matter-of-fact relationship with his clients. The second accountant signed up clients more gradually. She was intentional and accurate. Upon first contact with a prospective client, she suggested they meet in person to enable her and the client to determine if they were a good fit for one another over a long-term business relationship. During the initial meeting, she queried potential clients about their values, aspirations, and aims. Her practice grew slowly.

As they grew, the ethos of each accountant's practice differed significantly. The first accountant lost clients about every five years, though he cultivated a steady stream of new clients to replace the previous relationships. His practice was steady, neither declining nor growing. He worked and remained efficient and accurate. The second accountant's practice continued to expand. She added new clients slowly, added fresh staff judiciously, and remained intentional and accurate. By mid-career, her client roster steadily increased year after year. She mentored new accountants, sharing essential skills such as how to develop strengths, listen effectively, and ask insightful questions. She emphasized the importance of building professional knowledge guided by the clients' needs. She personally took time to reflect on her experience as an accountant and business owner to discern what new professional knowledge she needed to seek out, what she should integrate into her practice, what she was learning from her clients, and how she needed to adapt. She taught workshops on how to create an individually mapped journey toward mastery in various areas of their field. Because she had created a culture of continuous professional learning for herself, she drew others to her. She was a reflective practitioner.

This scenario is more of a case study than the actual recounting of events. The case study dynamics are designed to illustrate two different approaches within the same profession. The first accountant maintained a practice over his career. The second accountant expanded her practice and included benefiting others in the profession. I advocate for an approach that both expands the profession and benefits others. Reflective practice can accomplish that result.

Reflective practitioners work in all professions. In fact, certain professions consider learning from experience essential to becoming competent in that field. For example, the field of medicine divides learning into two segments: classroom instruction and clinical training. Learning the fundamentals and principles is the primary focus of classroom learning. Applying the fundamentals and principles to actual patients is the focus of clinical learning.

Clinical practice is different. Medical residents, for example, treat patients' symptoms, take medical histories, identify personal care habits, consult with families involved in patient care, and evaluate how likely a patient is to comply with treatment protocols. The patient treatment is multi-dimensional. Because treatment responses vary among individuals and families can aid or complicate treatment, a wise resident comes to understand that practicing medicine is both a science and an art. A few other professions, such as law, teaching, and nursing, require a two-tiered process: classroom learning to develop the fundamentals, and applying those fundamentals in real-life practice.

More often, a newly graduated professional moves directly into a job equipped with little more than the acquired body of academic knowledge. A new hire will not yet be well-versed in the complexity of their field. Some employees acquire this knowledge through trial and error, while others undertake a personal course of intentional learning. Regardless of the approach, for learning to be effective, the new hire must make time to reflect on past actions.

A reflective practitioner is someone who embraces the opportunity to use experience to learn. Learning takes place as the immediate experience becomes an object of curiosity and reflection. The immediate experience can also be with a chosen focus of spiritual, personal, vocational, or leadership development. Over time, integrating these multiple perspectives into the reflection yields the deepest learning. The reflective practitioner asks, "What questions arise from my most recent actions, and where might I find the answers? Did I intend this impact and result? Why or why not? Why do things in this organization happen the way they do?" Learners are curious. Discerning. Open to awe. "How did I get in the way? What did I do that hit the nail on the head? What would I do differently? What do I need to learn for the next situation? What do I need to repeat?"

Reflective practitioners also seek out individuals who can serve as role models in their chosen field. They integrate professional and vocational growth with personal and spiritual growth. Not every situation will have the exact same set of conditions. Yet future situations will share some similarities and require the application of acquired knowledge in new ways. Other future situations will require adaptive thinking in response to unfamiliar conditions. For these reasons, becoming a reflective practitioner is preparing to navigate the unknown.

The attributes of a reflective practitioner are a natural fit for someone in the practice of ministry. Developing reflective habits seems especially important as one begins her or his ministry. And indeed, the initial years of a clergy person's practice in ministry are known as formation (another term for reflective practice). Formation occurs in any environment as the new clergy person applies their academic foundation of the vocation to the spiritual lives of people. Formation is a critical component of clergy development. Research has shown that when the formation experience is negative—meaning it does not contribute to a healthy practice of ministry—then that clergy person is likely to leave the ministry within five years. Research also shows that when the formation is positive, the clergy person often remains in ministry for many years. What is more, on any given day, a priest is called upon to complete a task or address an issue that requires him or her to rely on their beliefs, personality traits, competence, inspiration, empathy, emotional intelligence, open heart, and financial know-how. The sort of positive formation within reflective practice enables the priest to learn and grow vocationally and personally, ensuring that he or she has abundant resources from which to draw.

Yet reflecting on experience as a learning method is not common in the ministry. A small number of natural learners exist who seek opportunities to gain personal, spiritual, and ministry-related experience. Experienced clergy who share their personal experiences of vocational growth can mentor newer clergy, inspiring them to reflective practice. Just as I navigated the unknown into a new stage of life while sailing our boat, *Soul Asset*, those who navigate the unknown by reflecting on their direct experience to grow spiritual leaders, I call learners of Soul Assets.

Soul Assets, intentionally plural, are the qualities of *perspective*, *wisdom*, *kindness*, *balance*, and *curiosity*. The vitality of Soul Assets depends upon continually learning from the direct experience of ministry—in other words, becoming a reflective practitioner over the duration of ministry (or other professional practice). Think back to the example of the accountants in this chapter's opening anecdote. One of them created and modeled a culture of continuous professional learning. That learning extended beyond classes to stay current with accounting practices, updates, and changes in the field. The learning encompassed personal and professional growth, supported others, and fostered development for both the leader and the business within the context of day-to-day accounting practice. The personal growth necessary for professional growth drew others to the accountant, both as a person and as a colleague.

Becoming a reflective practitioner begins with learning from experience. Too often, merely *having* the experience is mistaken for *learning* from the experience. Anyone can repeat the same action and get the same result each time. Reflective practitioners reflect on their experience to either change or confirm their earlier actions. They could intentionally seek different results.

But what does it look like to reflect on an experience to change an action?

During a conversation that feels confusing, a reflective practitioner will pause and intentionally reflect on the confusion and the resulting action. The pause may be a moment or a request for time to think things over. This pause for reflection opens the door to new actions that better fit the context and needs of the situation. The reflective practitioner determines which new action to test as an experiment. This is one phase of the reflective learning cycle.

Once the new action is tested, the result becomes the experience that is the subject of the next reflection. While the full process of reflective practice encompasses other components, such as mentors and peer learning, which are described in chapter 5, this action-reflection-action cycle is known as the Adult Learning Cycle.

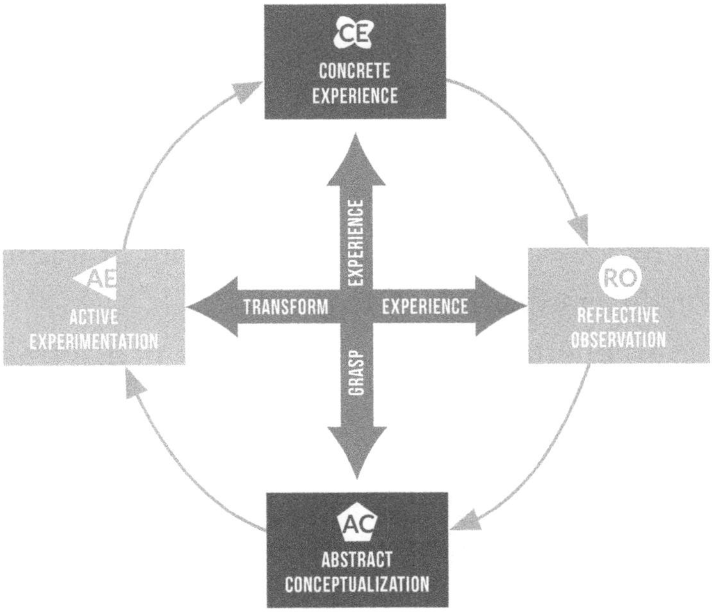

Figure 3.1: The Adult Learning Process cycle: Action-Reflection-New Action-Reflection, as developed by David Kolb.

Adult Learning Cycle

The Adult Learning Cycle was developed by David Kolb, who is best known for his research on experiential learning and learning styles (*Experiential Learning Experience as the Source of Learning and Development*, Pearson Education, 2015). In the cycle shown above—it's also known as the "Experiential Learning Cycle"—the learner progresses through all four quadrants. Ideally, the learner enters at the top, with the actual concrete experience, and then moves around clockwise. The Adult Learning Cycle describes an individual learner. As I offer examples and exercises in this chapter, I begin at the top of the cycle with the actual experience. I also engage a full community process of learners. While reflective practice can and is done by an individual, I believe that the multiple perspectives of a group, a peer learning community, is a more powerful way to access the depth of learning from direct experience.

An important characteristic of the peer learning community I am using as an example is that there is no designated facilitator or leader. The group consists of peers in a similar stage of ministry with similar questions. One person describes an experience that includes actions of self and others, thoughts, feelings, and questions. That person describing the event is the presenter. The role rotates in the group. The presenter in a peer learning community begins at the top of the cycle, describing the Concrete Experience.

However, a learner may enter at any quadrant and then proceed clockwise. For example, a learner may enter at the Reflective Observation stage. This most likely means the learner is reflecting on another person's experience. Then the cycle moves to Abstract Conceptualization, then Active Experimentation, and then Concrete Experience, when the learner personally engages with the experience. This is the process of the peer participants in a peer learning community. The peers are then "Observers" offering different perspectives of Abstract Conceptualization and generating more ideas for Active Experimentation.

The presenter then chooses an action to test and moves into another Concrete Experience, this time with changes to their actions that will make the experience different. The cycle begins again. And the learning continues.

The Adult Learning Cycle is a continuous, four-step cycle of learning that may become increasingly complex with practice and as the learner engages multiple levels. The key is that the learner passes through each step. This learning model is intentionally adaptable. First, it can be used with any focus, and the learner(s) determine the focus. Next, while the cycle describes one learner, its adaptability allows it to be used by a group. Finally, the learner(s) may enter the cycle at any point.

When we think about a sailor, the first thing a sailor feels is the wind in the sail and how to adjust the sail to that pressure. The second thing the sailor feels is the pressure of the water on the rudder and how to move the tiller to adjust the direction of the boat, which changes the pressure of the wind on the sails. That change in direction with the rudder changes the direction and speed of the boat. A beginner sailor may hold the sail tightly in one position and try to adjust the boat by moving the rudder. While this is possible, it is clunky. The degree of boat shift is usually over or under what is needed. The impact is a wild ride.

Adjusting the sail is a more precise, yet more skilled, adjustment that yields a smoother ride. The sail, wind, lines, sailor, rudder (and tiller moving the rudder), are all necessary to move the boat along the direction of navigation, never a straight line, while aiming for as close to a straight line as possible. Skilled sailing takes constant actual experience, reflecting on the experience, imagining abstract ideas of what might be better, choosing one to try, and then actually trying it. In sailing, all this happens quickly because wind and water conditions constantly change. The sailor learns about how to sail in these conditions through the experience of sailing in the conditions.

The same is true in the practice of ministry. Clergy and lay leaders learn ministry through the experience of offering ministry in actual contexts with real people in real changing conditions. Clergy bring in-depth theological training integrated into real contexts in changing conditions, and lay leaders bring professional experience integrated in the same way.

While David Kolb described how adults learn through experience, Malcolm Knowles, an earlier researcher and teacher, made an important contribution that explains *why* adults learn. Knowles authored the first edition of *The Adult Learner* in 1973 and made two important distinctions. The first is between education and learning. Knowles defines education as "an activity undertaken or initiated by one or more agents that is designed to effect changes in knowledge, skill, and attitudes in individuals, groups, or communities." The emphasis here is on the agent as the driver of the change, choosing the content intended to effect it. On the other hand, learning "emphasizes the person in whom the change occurs or is expected to occur." Here, the emphasis is on the act of learning and the individual undergoing the "behavioral change, knowledge, skills, and attitudes." In this definition, the learner is the driver of the content that delivers the change.[1]

It can also be said that a process imposed or engaged in may influence learning. Consider an earlier point that the early years of ministry formation may have been either positive or negative for a spiritual leader.

1. Malcom S. Knowles, Elwood F. Holton, and Richard A. Swanson, *The Adult Learner, Fifth Edition: The Definitive Classic in Adult Education and Human Resource Development* (Gulf Publishing, 1998), 11.

Negative experiences result in negative formation, which, according to an analysis by David Wood,[2] leads clergy to leave the ministry. Negative formation can be mitigated in certain situations, assuming one learns from failure. Positive experiences lead to healthy formation, which in turn leads clergy to continue serving in ministry for many years. Positive experience calibrates challenge and support. Positive experiences set standards for behavior within the vocation and reflect holistic and individual learning needs. Knowles coined a new term—*andragogy*—for a kind of learning that distinguishes adults from youth and views adults as agents of their own changes in behavior, knowledge, attitudes, and skills. As the opposite of pedagogy, andragogy means learners are now self-directed adults asking their own questions. Adults are most interested when they discover what they want or need to know. They are less interested in a pedagogical model where the expert tells them what they need to know.

Another characteristic of an adult is being responsible for their own decisions, their own lives. Adults need to be competent. Recall the last time you entered a new

2. David J, Wood was the project director of Transition into Ministry—the original grant program funded by the Lilly Endowment. David, Jim Wind of the Alban Institute, and Craig Dykstra, President of the Religion Division of the Lilly Endowment, worked together on this research before launching the Transition into Ministry Initiative. David made a presentation based on the research at the first Transition into Ministry Program Conference in the Spring of 2001.

place, and the signage was poor, or the directions were mumbled, or something that should be simple was made so overly complicated that you could not complete a simple action. Chances are, you were frustrated, maybe even mad, embarrassed, and feeling incompetent because the information you had did not help to point you in the desired direction. Adults seek answers in order to be responsible and to have agency in their lives.

Other characteristics of adult learners are:

—incorporating varied levels of experience into their competence
—learning to cope with real-life situations
—orienting their learning to what will answer their life-centered, problem-centered, or task-centered questions
—responding to their internal motivations for learning

For instance, consider that one priest may come to ministry with extensive experience in pastoral counseling and need more experience in preaching. Her subject matter and situations would be different from those of another priest who needs to develop his own preaching voice. He needs opportunities to preach in different styles and situations so he can test his preaching experience and reflect on it. Yet the inner core characteristics are the same for these two clergy learners.

Reflective Practice for Navigating Now: Individual Ministry Leader

The process outlined below assumes a discussion will take place within a community of peer learners/leaders. Individual learners/leaders could also use the process as a reflective exercise, although they should be aware that none of us can ever see our blind spots. A mentor with whom you can be truthful and who will tell you the truth can be a helpful conversation partner. Peer communities and mentors are described more in chapter 5.

Action

- Describe the situation, set the context.
- What do your peers need to know to "see" the situation?
- Describe the dynamics involved (e.g., emotional, social, historical, relational, conflict style, communication style).
- What action did you take?

Reflection

- How do you feel about the action in this situation? What is the emotion?

- Did you feel this anywhere in your body? What is the somatic reflection?
- What is personally challenging in this scenario?
- What is challenging in your ministry?
- Is there a challenge or adaptation for the parish that you can identify?
- What are you seeking from your peers?
- What feedback/insights/comments do you want from your peers?

New action

- What do you want to do differently?
- What would help you to experiment with a new action?
- What might you need to stop doing?
- What do you want to learn to deepen self-awareness, your ministry skills, or a specific skill? What did you identify that you could learn?
- What do you seek in a Connecting Conversation with God, with trusted others?
- When will you get back to our learning community about the action you tried?

- How do you want your peers to hold you accountable?
- What else do you want to know from your peers? What questions do you have that will help you reflect on the situation?

Action

- Describe the impact of the new action.
- What is the new situation?
- Repeat from the top of the cycle.

Reflective Practice: Peer Community Members

After the presentation by the individual member, each peer learner/leader considers:

- What did you hear in the presentation?
- Have you experienced a comparable situation or action?
- Consider the action from your peers' perspectives. Remember that the goal is not to solve a problem with one suggestion. What are the alternative approaches and points of view to consider?

- Where might you, as a peer learner, continue to be curious, and where might the presenter continue to be curious?
- In this situation, what feedback would you like to receive?
- Listening to your peer, what would you like to give?
- Consider the possibilities of stopping, continuing, and changing action.
- Suggest an action to test.
- As a result of this conversation, what do you want to do differently in your practice of ministry?

Reflective Practice: An Initial Exploration

- Choose a recent situation that you would like to explore for insight and learning. To get started, you might:
- Explore a recent conversation you had with another church leader about a meeting that turned in an unexpected direction.
- Consider a key volunteer who is consistently overpromising and underdelivering, and

think through the next conversation with this individual.

- Your colleague repeatedly comes to you with the same issue in his parish, and you listen patiently each time. However, the next time the colleague starts talking about the issue, you want to have a different response. Consider listening to your colleague as the presenter of the peer group, and your job is to generate as many new perspectives as possible. What would you say?
- Or consider you are having the same issue as your colleague. How would you present the issue to a group of peers, and what feedback would you like to receive?

Take yourself through these steps:

- Write out your responses.
- What action do you want to test?
- Walk through the conversation steps with a mentor or coach.
- What additional perspectives did you gain?
- What next actions did you decide to test?

The process above offers a framework for a reflective practice conversation. Consider this an invitation to form a peer-learning community of trusted colleagues who are at a stage of ministry like your own. Could you invite four to six colleagues to test the reflective practice conversation together?

As mentioned in the previous chapter, a mentor can be an extraordinary addition to a peer learning community. Members of an existing group can invite an experienced mentor to facilitate the group learning process. Or a mentor could form a peer-learning community for those at a specific stage of ministry. Mentoring for learning are the waters we navigate in the chapters ahead.

Becoming a Reflective Practitioner

The reflective practice model described above is designed to initiate a conversation within a peer group. It is possible to meet once a month, engage the model, go home, and re-engage at the next meeting. I adapted the adult learning model to foster peer-group conversations focused on a context and topic that were engaging and informative for all participants.

It is equally possible to integrate the model into an ongoing reflection every day. Reflective practice was originally described as an individual endeavor. Both

Kolb and Knowles refer to the individual adult learner. Their image is an individual adult moving through her or his professional life, learning, rather than an individual student sitting in a classroom; the individual is sitting in the experience of the moment. Two of my favorite sayings are, "You are the experiment" and "You are the laboratory."

An early contribution to opening the mechanics of reflective practice was Donald A. Schön's *The Reflective Practitioner: How Professionals Think in Action.*[3] As an M.I.T. professor of urban studies and education and a consultant, he compared five professions to uncover how professionals solve problems. He revealed that professionals rely less on what they learned in graduate school and more on what they learn in practice. He unwraps their thinking process to illustrate how reflection works and to foster its creative use for future professionals. The emphasis is on the individual reflecting on a problem or issue to further resolve it.

Sometimes a supervisor needs to reframe the question to make the problem more apparent. Rather than asking, "Why did you do it this way when you can see it didn't work?" a supervisor might ask, "Did other solutions occur to you in the process?" or "Can you identify a place you need help?" Sometimes an individual arrives at a solution by evaluating the range of experimental

---

3. Donald A. Schön, *The Reflective Practitioner: How Professionals Think in Action* (Basic Books, 1984).

approaches they have considered. In doing so, they draw on their experience and the specific circumstances of the situation. Thus, the individual learns from each problem-solving experience, incorporates the new knowledge into their information base, and draws on this expanded foundation when addressing future professional challenges.

Basically, this is the Adult Experiential Learning Cycle as employed by individual practitioners to think through situations unfamiliar in their realm of experience or situations novel in their field. These practitioners are navigating the unknown. Since Schön, others in Organizational Development have employed reflective practice as a tool to enhance job performance or educational outcomes.

It is often left up to the individual to develop this habit. I find this somewhat ironic since one must read a book about experiential learning and reflective practice and then practice the exercises to learn what it means to be a reflective practitioner. Reflective practice is not currently a habit, professional capability, or active model that a spiritual leader could learn in context from another leader. Yet experiential learning is a subject that focuses on learning from immediate experience. And, if it is to be used for professional, vocational, or personal growth, then some broad guidelines, along with practice groups, might be helpful.

I discovered a big-picture guideline in the publication *Creating the Reflective Habit: A Practical Guide for Coaches, Mentors, and Leaders* by Michelle Lucas.[4] Her book is a collection of articles by various reflective practitioners. She began her search for ways to initiate reflective practice, and the only method she found was journaling. Since she was never consistent at keeping a journal, she compiled additional practices that offer cognition, auditory, kinesthetic, visual, and even poetry as prompts.

To provide her readers with a basic understanding of reflective practice, Lucas establishes a clear definition. She describes reflective practice as "an iterative, open-ended, creative process where we take deliberate conscious time to explore and interrogate our practice in a systematic and systemic way."[5] This definition captures the curiosity shaped by questions relevant to immediate actions and the time needed not to wonder and wander, but to reflect on them toward possible solutions. And, as I have mentioned regarding conversations and adult learning, the process is highly intentional.

The opening chapter of Lucas's book also outlines helpful characteristics of what a reflective habit is. Again, the writers are drawing from information from across their fields. The author of one particular article

---

4. Michelle Lucas, *Creating the Reflective Habit, A Practical Guide for Coaches, Mentors, and Leaders* (Routledge, 2023).

5. Hannah Butler, "Understanding the Territory of Reflective Practice," *Creating the Reflective Habit, A Practical Guide for Coaches, Mentors, and Leaders* (Routledge, 2023), 4.

takes an example from an educator's comment that reflective practice "makes links between practice and the development of practice; connects the cognitive, emotional, and active elements; supports structured or organized thinking; takes place within various time zones (past, present, and future); illuminates our strengths; [and] is a way of identifying and working with our triggers."[6]

These characteristics echo the questions one can ask through the Adult Learning Cycle or reflective practice. However, the Adult Learning Cycle does not address cumulative impact. The cycle repeats itself from action to reflection, abstract ideas, and experimentation. The cycle assumes that along the way, the learner integrates the new information from the experimentation. One of the finer distinctions in the above list makes is "practice and the development of practice." As the learner integrates the new experiential information, future actions arise and are tested from a deeper base of experience. The cycle is not a one-time event. Rather, repetition builds into a pattern of thinking, observing, reflecting, and learning. This pattern develops into a reliable, repeating practice for drawing from previous experience, observing, approaching problems, discovering solutions, and incorporating new knowledge. An understood and assumed characteristic of reflective practice is that coaches, mentors, and leaders bring to the

6. Ibid.

people they serve ways of thinking and growing found in a wide variety of professions. Reflective practice itself is an integrative practice "discovered" independently by professionals as they seek ways to use direct experience to move forward.

Over my years in parish ministry, when clergy are frustrated by issues in the parish or intractable parish members, the conversation becomes "Isn't it awful." It's awful that this person always holds up a vestry decision by raising a new issue. It's awful that the same person keeps working out the same issue. It's awful, we can never solve the lawn mowing, or the organ repairs, or . . . fill in the blank. Because we see no solution, too often we become content with accepting that it is awful.

Reflective practice does not accept "Isn't it awful." An inner conversation with yourself, or better yet, with a mentor, framing the problem or issue so that potential experimental solutions can emerge, is one step away from accepting the awful. Looking at your question through a personal, spiritual, historical, organizational, or communication lens is another step away from accepting awful. Setting a personal goal of learning from what seems like an intractable situation by connecting the practice of ministry with developing a practice of ministry (getting better at what you do) gives the priest agency. Using your experience to practice your reflective habit is another step in exercising agency. Inviting others to be peers in the process is yet another.

This is a new way for clergy to approach ministry development. That is why I refer to it as ministry practice. It is ongoing and daily, and can occur in small, informal moments, such as taking notes and listening, or in deliberate, conscious time set aside to reflect on specific questions. It can be theological, pastoral, and personal all at once. You learn about yourself, allow others to learn about you, and gain insight into the people you're speaking with. This creates a deeper, more meaningful conversation than one that ends with simply complaining about current problems.

You will gain from the practice what you bring to it. The more you practice intentionally reflecting, the more likely you are to learn.

Reflective Practice and Spiritual Life

In chapter 1, "Connecting," I wrote about mindfulness and Centering Prayer. They share in reflective practice. Both mindfulness and Centering Prayer are ways of being conscious. Mindfulness is being conscious of the present moment. Centering Prayer involves consciously letting go, allowing one to rest in the arms of God. These two pathways bring the practitioner to a different place of consciousness. Mindfulness is not prayer. And while Centering Prayer is a form of meditation, the focus of attention is not the present moment but the presence of God. These two ways of consciousness share with reflective practice the necessity of cultivating consistent practice. To retrain our minds from the usual jumping from thought to thought to emotion to distraction, we *practice* mindfulness, we *practice* Centering Prayer.

As we cultivate our minds to return to the moment, to return to the openness for God, also known as listening for God, we build our ability to engage in reflective practice. Consider setting aside intentional time to consciously reflect in an organized way on a particular action as another form of "sit" that shapes your ministry. This is not a substitute for your prayer practice or meditation practice. This is a healthy habit to live and minister among your community and household. It is a health habit to improve your self-awareness, your understanding of ministry, your information about what might be done, and your preparation to navigate the unknown. Reflective practice is also the spiritual practice of a lively, growing friendship with Jesus. Consider friendship with Jesus as an embodied presence of Jesus. We say we are called to be Jesus' hands and feet in the world. We are called to act on Jesus' behalf, to act in our present time now as he teaches. Action is one form of embodiment.

Friendship is another form of embodiment. When we are friends, we understand our friends more deeply than in other relationships, and yet, given our human limitations, we never completely know them. And our human friends deeply understand us and yet never know us completely. Sometimes, a friend knows us better than we know ourselves, offering perspective when we most need it. Friendship's expression is a unique combination of companionship, kindness, compassion, affection, generosity, autonomy, values that shape our lives, commitments, history, communication, and rituals.

Christ calling us friends offers a relationship that is uniquely ours—shaped by our own particular blend of companionship, kindness, compassion, affection, thirst for justice, longing for peace, generosity, autonomy, and the values that guide our lives. It is a relationship rooted in commitment, history, communication, and ritual—an inexhaustible source of meaning in our lives and across generations.

Jesus calls us into friendship in our perfect imperfection, with our strengths and weaknesses. Our "full package" comes together as a friend of Jesus so that we may, in our bodies and with our spirits, offer that friendship to others.

We are named by Jesus as his friends in his farewell address. He no longer expects the disciples at the table with him, or the disciples who follow them, or any of the later generations of disciples, to simply repeat his words. The relationship with Jesus and his teaching is much more intimate than information. The intimate relationship is daily living with Jesus and Jesus living within us. One could say it "gets under your skin." Or Jesus' Way of Life becomes part of you.

I did not live in the first century, so I cannot fully appreciate how those first disciples expressed that call, that charge, by Jesus to be his friends. I do not know their context, their personal histories, the reflections and options that arose as they made choices in the way of Jesus' life. They honored his life by living by his teachings. I can only read about what they did, their histories, and what others have said, to get as close to their experience as possible.

I cannot have their experience, nor can they have mine. In my context, in my generation, on this day, I am a different friend of Jesus. Since no two experiences can ever be the same and should not be the same, each charge from Jesus to be a friend thankfully brings forth unique characteristics. And there are enough commonalities across these experiences for Jesus' friends to gather to learn with and from one another, to give thanks together, and to worship the holy sacredness of His life. At the same time, we also recognize the small and yet ultimately significant way it is embodied in our own way of life.

We are named by Jesus as his friends so that we may live a life of continuous learning: respecting one another, acting for the benefit of one another, seeking the best in ourselves, and desiring the best for others. Our intentions flourish through the sharing of Christ's life within and among us. This is the reflective practice of continuous learning by loving one another.

The accountant, as a reflective practitioner in the opening story, developed long-term relationships with her clients for her growth, their benefit, and the well-being of her mentees. To me, this is lay ministry. As ministers of the sacraments, can we create a ritual with John 15:12-17 as the reading?

> This is my commandment, that you love one another as I have loved you. No one has greater love than this, to lay down his life for one's friends. You are my friends if you do what I command you. I do not call you servants any longer, because the servant does not know what the master is doing, but I have called you friends, because I have made known to you everything that I have heard from my Father. You did not choose me, but I chose you. And I appoint you to go and bear fruit, fruit that will last, so that the Father will give you whatever you ask him in my name. I am giving you these commandments so that you may love one another.

Prayers could be offered as an individual begins a new job, undertakes a business venture, sends off a manuscript, asks blessings for an ongoing profession, faces challenges to their profession, such as recent challenges to lawyers, law enforcement, ethics officers, food pantry directors, and dedicated volunteers. We pray for these important members of our social fabric in the Prayers of the People, mentioning them in a single sentence. Perhaps a ritual, a sermon, or a reflection—a teaching, a laying on of hands to strengthen them for navigating the unknown would affirm their friendship with Jesus in the world. Or, offering affirmation for lay ministry could be at the beginning or at the end of a reflective practice training to offer to God "ourselves, our souls, and bodies." (The Book of Common Prayer, 336) For members of our churches, how do we celebrate their reflective practice as friends of Jesus?

As ordained ministers, might we claim this straightforward approach to our own reflective practice—a friendship with Jesus as we navigate the unknown? Jesus gave his disciples the charge, "I do not call you servants any longer, because the servant does not know what the master is doing; but I have called you friends because I have made known to you everything that I have heard from my Father." Friends who know one another well enough can say what Jesus means and live to reflect his life. Even with an adult's self-directed need to discover for ourselves what that life together looks like, we can nevertheless claim our own unique experiences and needs that we bring to a life in Christ.

Perhaps it is necessary to say that this is a deeper, more profound friendship with a pal with whom we share interests, sports, food, books, music, time together, and organizations. This is a friendship in which we commit ourselves as learners to be agents of our own change, drawing on the inner resources of Christ's life within and the outer resources of scripture, the church, reason, and experience. As we navigate the unknown in ministry practice, just as we do with friends in Jesus, we act, deeply explore, trust, and take risks. In the process, we share in the change we need now, and the world needs now.

CHAPTER 4

Stages of Ministry and Reflective Practice

Let the same mind be in you that was in Christ Jesus.

—Philippians 2:5

The complexity of understanding a rector's role and integrating a lay leader's role is often complicated by assumptions we all too easily make. A rector served a church that, prior to the rector's arrival, had overextended the congregation's capacity on a building project. Confident that the new project would bring in more people, the leadership pushed ahead. Now, growth was disappointing, the spreadsheets were disappointing, and stewardship was disappointing because a significant portion of the congregation was still mad about the project. The vestry struggled through several monthly meetings. Finally, the treasurer, a successful businessman and accountant, pronounced at a meeting, "The purpose of this church is to bring more people in so that they will pledge!" To which the rector responded, "The purpose of this church is to bring people to Christ."

From the treasurer's point of view, he spoke from his experience, but the idea that the purpose of the church was to only capture people for their money fell flat. Members sought to be much more than a financially smooth-running business.

From the rector's point of view, if the church's mission was not to bring people to Christ, then the church could be any not-for-profit offering programs that helped people and, in this case, educated children. Yet most of the business leaders were looking for a financially smooth-running organization.

What if long before the congregation forged ahead with a building plan, they had talked about integrating a smooth-running and financially solvent organization with the foundations of a Christian community? How could business leadership have stretched itself to understand the odd mix of uneven cash flow in a church (most of the money collected in December) with an elusive "product" of relationships? What if the previous rector discussed business theologically, not in terms of transactional return on investment, but in terms of return on lives enriched, expanded, and more deeply faithful? These are concepts that could stretch each conversation partner. A spiritual leader serving in this congregation would need to develop competency with theological concepts and faith community dynamics. A rector serving in this congregation would need to develop a competency in the strengths of a business mindset, translating theological concepts, and distinguishing the specific missions of different types of organizations.

A Stages of Ministry Practice for the Ordained Leaders and the Lay Leaders offers a map for forming and understanding one another as leaders heading to the same point on the shore.

In dynamic leadership situations, the four-part process of reflective practice, outlined in the previous chapter, involves a continuous cycle: beginning with the actual experience of an action, moving to observation and reflection on that action with self and peers, progressing to the development of new abstract concepts for possible actions, and culminating in testing a new action experience. This final step returns the practitioner to the start of the cycle, creating an ongoing pathway for learning from current experience.

When situations are sufficiently different and changing rapidly from what has happened before, no single right answer exists. Adaptive leadership is built on a simple premise: experimentation drives adaptation. In a world where leaders face new situations every day, learning from fresh experiences becomes essential. Leadership is a continual process of navigating unfamiliar waters and shifting dynamics. The challenge, then, is knowing whether the adjustments a leader makes truly address the realities of the moment or help set a steady long-term course. Effective experience requires both testing and fine-tuning.

Sailors know that sailing is not finding that one point of sail on the horizon, setting the sails, and then never needing to adjust the sails again. Sailors know sailing is always adjusting. When you sit in a sailboat, nothing else sits still (unless, of course, there is no wind, and then the boat does not move). When you sit in a sailboat, the wind, the waves, and the tide all put different levels of pressure on the sails, the hull of the boat, the rudder, and the bow. The sailor primarily adjusts the wind pressure on the sail, better described as the wind speed over the sail, the same as the wind speed over the wing of an airplane. While the sail adjusts to the wind, the pressures on the other parts of the boat also influence how the boat moves. The flow of wind and water naturally varies from moment to moment. The sailor is constantly making small or larger adjustments to keep moving toward the same point of sail, that chosen point on the horizon. An experienced sailor learns by testing how much adjustment to make in some conditions and how little adjustment to make in others.

The practice of ministry is like a sailboat that is always moving with the naturally varying levels of wind and water. To me, this is the adventure, fun, and joy of ministry. A new sailor will require a lot of testing, experimenting with different wind pressures on sails, and creating the forward momentum of the boat. A more experienced sailor uses the accumulated knowledge of moving forward in a wide range of conditions and is willing to take more risks. A new sailor is less flexible; an experienced sailor is more flexible.

The stage of ministry from which a clergy or lay leader is working can greatly shape their flexibility with process, their engagement in reflective practice, and their development as a reflective practitioner.

The heart of clergy vocational development is integrating theoretical academic knowledge with practical experience. Academic study is the pedagogy of ministry. Traditionally, experts, knowledgeable professors, some of whom are also clergy with congregational experience, teach the context that forms the foundation of ministry. These experts in the theological school determine the essential content for earning the required Master of Divinity degree. Most denominations prescribe standards for this academic content, as well as for the prospective minister's ability to demonstrate competent mastery of it.

Paths other than a three-year residential theological education are also emerging. Some seminaries that previously offered only full-time residential programs now sponsor primarily online classes with only a short, annual residential component. Others offer only online classes and no longer maintain academic buildings or campus infrastructure. Some theological schools make it possible for an MDiv candidate to take classes while continuing their current full-time employment without relocating a spouse and family to pursue a degree. In other situations, a region or diocese may partner with a seminary for some parts of the theological curriculum and develop other parts of the program locally.

The effectiveness of each pedagogical model remains a topic of debate, as religious institutions try to balance the need to provide theological education for the diverse individuals God calls to ministry with the expectations of many that a certain amount of residential formation is required for theological students preparing for ministry. Conversations continue to discern what is lost and what is gained in the different pathways, but the foundation of academic pedagogy informs the needs and questions of everyone who seeks to learn from their experience. It is the foundation that the pedagogical learner gathers in expert-determined learning that the adult learner integrates into their self-determined learning through practical experience. The academic foundation significantly shapes how the emerging adult learner engages new situations and contexts.

Clinical Pastoral Education (CPE) and Supervised Field Education (Field Ed) offer opportunities for learning from experience during the academic formation process. However, the self-reflective process of CPE and the goals to be completed in Field Ed are determined by the supervisors. The learner is not yet an adult learner with the agency to form questions and the responsibility for his or her own learning.

New clergy launch into their context with deep intellectual formation and initial formation in ministry practice. The "watch the gap" narrative earlier in the book illustrates how different clergy understand what is happening and what is needed. Not surprisingly, the new priest is ready to take on full agency. Equally not surprising, the institution relies on what it knows best, an academic model. Here we have another gap.

Fortunately, other vocations and professions recognize a continuum of professional development that offers insight into clergy development. Nursing is one such profession (as well as a vocation). Nurses enter clinical practice with a deep theoretical foundation and basic practical skills. They mirror the ways clergy develop through the contextual experience that is gained as participants in an increasingly complex human decision-making context.

When my daughter graduated from college, she gathered with three of her closest high school friends. Each of them majored in very different fields: sociology, business, psychology, and nursing. They discussed graduate work and what a future profession could look like. They wondered how they would know what they truly wanted to study, where they could make a difference, and whether they would feel as strongly about their choice after ten years in practice.

I was honored when these young women asked me to join their conversation, which was fundamentally about vocation and profession. The nursing student attended a well-recognized university with a top-notch research hospital. Her passionate interest was pediatric oncology. Two weeks before the group met, she began her first nursing job at the university hospital as a pediatric oncology nurse. Clearly, she felt that her profession was also her calling, deep in her bones. I asked her what knitted the two together.

She recounted her first week on the job. She knew she had the technical skill to take care of a kid with cancer. She also knew she did not have a nuanced understanding of treatments, side effects, the role of family as supporters or detractors of treatment, and very early signs of emotional changes—the ones nurses are always the first to notice. Right away, she observed how the other nurses on the floor did their jobs. She chose two experienced nurses from whom she wanted to learn. She approached each privately and said, "I want to be a nurse just like you. Would it be alright if I watched you?"

What knit her together with each model was her continual learning and reflection on her life as a pediatric oncology nurse. There were nuances she would learn in the act of nursing. And there were personal characteristics she might need to develop, such as listening skills. Another personal characteristic—her exuberant laugh—had already been a strength in social settings. She realized it could also be a strength at work if she learned to be a little less uninhibited. Laughter was still heartfelt and appropriate for her, even a little dialed back.

These are not personal reflections anyone makes easily. I was greatly impressed by her maturity in examining herself and her vocation together, which allowed her to grow in both areas. She translated this mature approach to her agency as a learner into becoming a reflective practitioner in her vocation.

This young woman's nursing skills deeply developed by adopting a mindset that continuous learning is an essential part of her profession. Nursing recognizes that academic training, combined with some clinical training, is the foundation of professional practice. Guides to increasing levels of complexity help nurses anticipate what lies ahead in their development and chart a course in that direction. As adult learners, each nurse is responsible for what he or she needs to effectively undertake their learning process. The profession also provides benchmark opportunities to test proficiency.

Nursing, along with other professions such as law and teaching, draws on the individual's direct experience for professional growth. Each field designates essential skills and competencies characteristic of ascending levels of proficiency. While professional certifications earned through continuing education are part of the complexity, the nuances and depth are built through reflective practice. There are other professions that also require the practitioner to build experience over the years, such as architecture, finance, and management.

Along with clergy, lay leaders can become reflective practitioners for their ministry in the church. They may already have a jump start as reflective practitioners in their respective fields of practice and expertise. The heart of lay leadership development is integrating the theoretical knowledge and learning from professional experience in a particular field with various aspects of a faith community. These include the faith community's theological principles, structure of governance, and the role of an affiliated national faith organization (if there is one). Integration of the lay leader also requires that they have a deep understanding of the faith community's interpersonal dynamics, clarity about the roles and responsibilities of the clergy leader and other lay leaders, and a robust understanding of the characteristics of the surrounding community.

I developed the Stages of Ministry Development described below from observations gathered through my reflective practice in ministry. The time spent in each stage is also based on my observations. The label for each stage is adapted from the Dreyfus Model of Skill Development.[1]

The Stages of Ministry

I use five categories for Ordained Ministry Practice and Lay Leader Ministry: Initial Year, Advanced Beginner, Competent, Proficient and Confident, and Experienced with Deep Understanding. Each category describes a certain level of skills and a range of experience expected. The years associated with each category also align with the experience base of most clergy, especially those in the first five years of ministry.

1. The Dreyfus Model of Skill Development proposes that a student passes through five distinct stages of novice, advanced beginner, competence, proficiency, and expertise.

Each stage is only representative. Because an individual's skill levels may differ, they may reasonably be placed in more than one category at the same time. For example, a newly ordained priest could be a beginner, having no prior professional experience, as they progressed from a bachelor's degree to a Master of Divinity and then to ordination. Or, if that priest entered the ministry from a counseling background, that person might be a beginner in some areas while also being proficient in relationship formation, understanding organizations, and working with families. In addition, when a clergy person enters a new context, they often become an Advanced Beginner, facing challenges such as time management as they adapt to a new context.

As we learn in our living, growing friendship with Christ, we become more aware of the mind of Christ within us. Over the course of a lifetime, we come to realize that Christ's love is our love in action in this moment. We notice virtues of humility, self-sacrifice, and obedience appearing within us, as Paul extols. Through my reflective practice, I appreciate the dynamic side of the mind of Christ. The actions I reflect on, clarify, take new action on, risk, test, and then reflect on again lead me forward through the unknown. Through accumulated learning from this process, I progress from each category to the next stage of my development.

Stages of Ministry of Ordained Practice

First Year—Initial Year

The newly ordained enters the context of practice knowing certain rules, but has not yet developed the skills needed to apply them. As a result, context-dependent judgment and skill are acquired through the experience of testing and challenging those rules.

- Clergy typically enter the parish or other ministry as ordained leaders with experience limited to the formal aspects of preaching, teaching, and pastoral care. New clergy often struggle to prioritize responsibilities because all ministerial activities are experienced with an equal level of importance. This process is further complicated by the dissonance between the theory of academic learning and the experience of learning from vocation.
- This dissonance can be the focus of reflective practice. New actions are often limited by possibilities that might only work within that clergy person's context. Reflective practice is a beneficial experience.

Second Year through Fifth Year of Ministry Practice: Advanced Beginner

A pastor at an advanced beginner level is functioning daily as an ordained, public, spiritual leader by preaching, teaching, conducting sacramental rites, supervising volunteers, and learning the history of the congregation (or institution) they serve. They have already encountered enough situations to recognize a pattern and culture emerging from this context. They are finding their own preaching voice, prioritizing time, constantly assessing the balance between vocation, family, rest, study, and play. During this period—typically the second to fifth years of ministry—they also navigate the challenges of fully transitioning into their call. They may begin to serve on diocesan committees or community organizations. They have higher hopes for their future ministry.

They are developing their own preaching voice, learning to prioritize their time, and continually evaluating the balance among vocation, family, rest, study, and play. They may begin taking on roles in diocesan committees or community organizations, and they often experience a growing sense of hope about their future ministry.

Reflective practice begins to build new learning. With more awareness of self in action, learning from experience feels more natural. With greater awareness of the various roles in ministry, the possibilities for learning expand.

Six to Ten Years of Ministry Practice: Competent

After repeatedly experiencing similar situations, ministry practice themes are becoming familiar. As the clergyperson relies on competence gained through experience, confidence grows. The clergy person and leader begin to see their actions in terms of long-range goals, learning needs, and plans.

- Clergy ordained for six to ten years are now conversant in constructing the foundational history and key dynamics of their current context. They are familiar with how effective lay leadership works, as well as the disappointments and delights of the congregation. They may also already have been able to influence the congregation's functioning, especially if a specific need was clearly stated at the time of their call. As the bigger picture of the parish comes into view, they may begin to serve on more complex diocesan committees or take on a more public role in community organizations. The clergy person is ready to try new styles of preaching, advance the deeper needs of the congregation, such as stewardship, governance, and staffing, and may be discerning how to serve in a more complex parish that requires learning new skills. At this point, some clergy still need to build greater flexibility to navigate multiple parish life crises without being overwhelmed.

- Reflective practice can be a creative approach to goals, learning, and plans. Especially in identifying learning needs, reflective practice reveals deeper levels to explore.

Ten through Fifteen Years of Ministry: Proficient and Confident

A proficient pastor understands situations as a whole system and stops trying to adhere to each action as a rule or maxim.

- A proficient clergy person moves from recognizing dynamics to shaping relationships, the parish community, and her leadership style with the comprehensive ministerial context in mind. This is a time of significant leadership development because the role of the clergy extends beyond self-definition and self-actualization to become an active definer of the congregation's vision, values, and character.
- The clergy person is ready to take risks, and vocational life is in a balanced flow. She can stretch herself when long work hours are needed to engage a crisis and can then refuel by temporarily handing over the responsibility and stepping back. Her preaching, teaching, pastoral care, and administrative output is consistent even as the needs in these areas fluctuate. She can supervise employees

and finances competently and may also begin to mentor new clergy. Clergy at this stage of development are calm in describing challenges and creative in seeking solutions.

Reflective practice becomes a natural part of self-guided growth, learning from experience, and peer discussion.

Fifteen Years of Ministry and Beyond: Experienced with Deep Understanding

An experienced clergy person possesses a substantial and varied professional background. The grasp of each situation is intuitive. It is no longer necessary to consider a wide range of options. Good potential approaches and solutions are sorted through in the context of pastoral experience, as a natural thought process. This intuitive grasp of each situation reflects a deep understanding that is nevertheless sometimes elusive for the clergy person to describe in words, and yet it is observable by others.

- While it is seldom possible for any clergy person, no matter how experienced, to grasp the total situation of shifting community life, an experienced clergy person engages her congregation with flexibility and fluidity that enables her to consistently have a balcony-level view of the congregation and an awareness of the daily dynamics of community life.

- Often these clergy are called to diocesan and/or national leadership positions. She may be recognized for a particular gift, e.g., preaching, spiritual writing, stewardship, administration, or innovation. She is conversant in connecting the biblical story with her personal story and the community's story. The vocation of self, family, church, and prayer is deeply integrated. The clergy person communicates the "core and counter-testimony" of life in faith: profound joy and full awareness of the suffering, injustice, and biases human beings visit on one another. Hope transcends suffering.
- Reflective practice cannot be separated from the clergy person's ongoing interest in deepening spirituality, connection, competency, and joy in ministry. The clergy person values ongoing reflective practice with peers.

Stages of Lay Leadership Ministry

The most significant distinction between lay and ordained leaders is that lay leaders already have a professional practice. They could be teachers, plumbers, lawyers, childcare experts (also known as homemakers), doctors, accountants, real estate salespeople, scientists, or mental health professionals. Lay leaders necessarily serve a faith community from a wide variety of backgrounds. They bring the skills of their profession and experience to their leadership role in the church. Lay leaders may begin serving in the faith community with considerable background knowledge of the community and a broad network of friends. Or they may arrive in a congregation with considerable professional knowledge but little background in the life of the community and a fledgling network of friends.

In contrast, ordained leaders serve a faith community as their profession and are paid for their time. They are also trained in the faith community's fundamental beliefs, values, and conduct.

Because the stages of lay leadership development do not unfold in the graduated years of experience cycles envisioned above, what follows is an ideal scenario. Often, lay leaders are engaged in church ministry by leveraging the competencies they already bring from their professions. What we might learn from this ideal, graduated progression is ways to integrate spiritual formation within lay leadership who have years of experience in church ministry.

First Lay Leadership—Initial Years

The new lay leader usually does not know and cannot be expected to know the rules, roles, and responsibilities. Therefore, they have not yet developed the skills needed to apply the rules or act confidently in the role. Beginner lay leaders may say that they will be silent for the first year observing how "things" are done. New lay leaders, particularly those serving in elected positions, may view their responsibility as representing the congregation against the clergy and other lay leaders perceived as in power. Establishing a collaborative leadership norm for everyone can be a responsibility of all leaders.

A beginner lay leader's experience with ordained clergy might be limited to the formal aspects of preaching, teaching, and pastoral care. New lay leaders may view clergy as "different" and wonder how to treat this "holy person." Creating diverse experiences across all levels of leadership expands possibilities.

There can also be a dissonance between the lay leader's expectation of the faith community and the inner workings of the month-to-month organization. And their sphere of competence is their profession, so in discussions, it is natural for the new lay leader to rely heavily on knowledge he or she already has.

Reflective practice helps reset expectations for self and others.

Three to Ten Years of Lay Leadership: Competent

After a range of experiences that repeat, the congregational themes are becoming familiar. The lay leader begins to view their actions in terms of long-range goals, learning needs, and plans for both the faith community and personal growth.

Lay leaders committed to learning about the faith community as a living organization become familiar with the foundational history and key dynamics of their congregation. They are familiar with lay leadership dynamics, both within themselves and among their current and past leaders. They understand the consequences of helpful decisions and unhelpful behavior. They experience the disappointments and delights of the congregation. They are also developing the skill to balance the many responses and opinions of the members who seek them out, including those with complaints. The Lay leader respects the good practice of "no surprises" for the rector. They are consistent in communicating their thoughts and opinions directly to the clergy leader and thoughtful in sharing information that the clergy person needs to act on. Since the lay leader is comfortable with the parish's bigger picture, they may begin serving on more complex diocesan committees.

Reflective practice identifies areas for learning and new interests associated with serving the faith community. Reflective practice can also help identify strengths for leadership.

Ten through Fifteen Years of Lay Leadership: Proficient and Confident

A proficient lay leader understands situations as a whole system and becomes an ally of the clergy and other leadership, an agent for change, and a listener. A proficient lay leader fully integrates knowledge of his or her profession with the comprehensive ministerial context. This is a time of significant leadership development, as the lay leader becomes an active co-definer of the congregation's vision, values, and character, in full collaboration with the clergy and other leaders. These lay leaders are calm in describing challenges and creative in seeking solutions.

Reflective practice continues to identify learning areas that expand and deepen.

Fifteen Years of Lay Leadership and Beyond: Experienced with Deep Understanding

An experienced lay leader has a broad background. Often these leaders are called to diocesan and/or national leadership positions. Or this lay leader may discern a new call to another profession, to train as a spiritual director, or to ordained ministry. She may be recognized for a particular gift, e.g., preaching, spiritual writing, stewardship, administration, or innovation. She is conversant in connecting the biblical story with her personal story, the community's story, and her professional story. Vocation, family, church, and prayer are deeply integrated. The lay leader communicates the "core and counter-testimony" of life in faith: profound joy and full awareness of the suffering, injustice, and biases human beings visit on one another. Hope transcends suffering.

Reflective practice focuses on specific experiences of joy, call, strengths, gifts, and ways to serve.

Exercise: Reflective Practice Process to the Stages of Ministry

Reflective Practice for Self-Awareness:

- Read each stage of ministry.
- Place yourself in the Stage that most represents where you are now.
- Engage the Reflective Practice for Navigating Now: Individual Ministry Leader in chapter 3, with the focus on your Stage.
- What Stage would you like to learn more about?

Reflective Practice for Peer Learners:

- Read each stage of ministry prior to the gathering.
- Share which stage of ministry most represents where you are now.
- Is there a range of Stages or a common overlap?
- What is the next Stage for each peer?
- Engage the reflective practice: Peer Community Members in chapter 3, with the focus on your current stage.

Living Libraries

Through reflective practice, we are living libraries for one another. Listening to experiences at the same stage of ministry offers multiple perspectives and generates new approaches to test. Listening to experiences that resonate also confirms that we are on common ground in our questions, frustrations, joys, and stumbling blocks. We may be surprised to discover we are not alone. Learning from experience expands when we can learn from several situations in addition to our own.

We are also living libraries for resources, the helpful book on a subject, and the support that makes experimentation possible. New knowledge, whether through study or experience, enters our ministry practice through rich pathways and our peers.

A significant contribution to leadership formation is that we are living libraries for one another as we gain self-awareness. We cannot know ourselves as an isolated person. We learn about ourselves through our relationships with others: how they perceive us, how we perceive them, and how those impressions shift. How do reactions bubble up, and what are the sources of those reactions? As we look deeper, we learn how to be in a relationship with ourselves.

One thing is sure in ministry practice—the good, kind, clear person we are trying to be is challenged when we make a necessary decision that another person does not like. Yet it is the leader's responsibility to make decisions. That challenge is a resource for learning more; however, we are seldom able to take a deep look into our inner selves on our own. Peers, coaches, mentors, therapists, and spiritual directors help when needed.

Most importantly, we are living libraries for one another in our relationship with God. As we move through the life of our ministry practice, so too does God move with us. We are changing, and God is right there. How do we describe the way in which that relationship is changing? With whom can we have that deep theological conversation that characterized the years of academic formation? Experiences, shifts, questions, feelings that arise from being present with people ask us, from time to time, to return to a theological foundation and then think through where we are *now* with God. Certainly, at those times, a spiritual director is a significant conversation partner. And a peer at the same stage of ministry can help us find words and feelings only accessible through shared experience.

A coach or mentor can be an extraordinary addition to a peer learning community. It may be that the coach forms a peer learning community for a specific stage of ministry. Or if the group is already formed, an experienced coach or mentor is invited to facilitate the group learning process.

CHAPTER 5

Mentors, Peers, and Learning Communities

You shall love the Lord your God with all your heart, and with all your soul, and with all your strength, and with all your mind; and your neighbor as yourself."

—Luke 10:27

Three seminary graduates intentionally committed to staying connected as they entered their first years of ministry. These three were friends, spiritual companions, and are now discovering how to grow as colleagues together. The bishop assigned one new priest to an urban parish with a long-standing rector. The new priest in a different diocese was assigned to a rural, parish with a long-standing rector about to retire. The Letter of Agreement stated that the new priest would serve as the interim when the rector retired. The third priest went to a suburban multi-staffed church. All three were in different dioceses. These three priests, at the beginning of their ministry, learned that connection with peers was essential because it could be the only connection for reflective-growth conversations.

The rectors and staff of these three parishes offered wide-ranging capabilities for reflecting on ministry with a new priest. The range began with no capabilities at all. For example, one new priest was called a "baby priest" as in one who knows nothing. At the other end of the spectrum sat the rector whose learning model was the basic model of observe, then do. This is a top-down model focused on the "right" way to do the functions in the parish. And it is the model most spiritual leaders in congregations know.

However, nowhere in that range was conversation about the history of the parish, curiosity about the new priest, or questions about how other priests learned, and what constituted important joys and celebrations. The familiar learning model did not include reflection on actions, meanings, protocols, vocation, personal growth, ministry stages, and the theology of ministry. Yet reflection on action is how adults learn.

These three new priests chose a process to reflect with one another and learned what they could from their conversations of curiosity and companionship. Sighting this point on the horizon, they could be a guiding navigation point for one another in these brand-new experiences. Further support could have been a guide with experience in these waters who could suggest what none of them could possibly know at these early stages of ministry, raise up protocols, establish a range of norms for the inevitable surprises that stretched their assumed norms, and call for time to pause and celebrate the joy. For these three new clergy, a mentor was not available. They began sorting out all these dynamics on their own as a reflective practice.

And each of these priests sailed these new waters with a congregation—a community already formed when the journey launched. A congregation can also be a partner in the learning cycle. Known as a Learning Congregation, with conversations and reflections designed to move forward toward growth for everyone, the new spiritual leader and existing members sail together with a shared point of navigation, a shared mission of spiritual leadership formation.

In the absence of another method, these three priests, as friends, created their own support system and learning community. This chapter describes a process by which clergy may choose a learning community designed to address learning needs at each stage. When congregations, experienced clergy, trained mentors, and collaborative diocese and seminaries look to the positive early formation of a new priest, tried and tested processes are available. Ideally, with the bishop's support, these programs take place within a congregation prepared for the ministry of forming new priests, with experienced clergy attuned to the challenges of the initial years of ministry, and trained mentors or coaches to support and challenge the priest and peer group along the way. There are several configurations of these programs, each bearing four key characteristics: a safe place to learn, involvement of the bishop, experienced clergy and mentors, and new clergy in a peer learning group for reflective practice.

Remember the Adult Learning Cycle by Kolb, described in chapter 3, is the foundation of reflective practice. Beginning with a concrete action, the reflective practitioner moves to the second step: observing and reflecting on the action. Peers can be essential here. The next step is for all participants to generate abstract ideas for a new action to try. The fourth step, to test the chosen action, moves the reflective practitioner back to the top of the cycle.

A key characteristic of adult learning is that adults tend to seek immediate new information to address the questions they currently have. In other words, they are not likely to read an entire book on the pastoral care of grieving family members when the question is how to care for a son with inconsolable grief for his mother. The first place they turn for information is a more experienced colleague with the question, "Have you ever experienced this, and if so, what did you do?" Another place to turn is the family, who can help you learn more about this young man in a sensitive way. Caring but curious questions can be asked about the relationship this person had with his mother and others: Are they concerned? Surprised? Is this a pattern?

This is the cycle of adult learning: action, reflection on the action, recognition of the need for new information before the next action, and then shaping the next action, incorporating the new information.

Most clergy have lots of questions. New clergy have so many questions, generated by the flood of new experiences, that they often feel as if they are drinking from a fire hose. This is a metaphor used by those new to a position when so much unfamiliar information comes all at once that they are overwhelmed. Imagine a safe place where the many questions are given voice or a time set aside to turn off the first hose. An aid to exploring the questions is an experienced clergy person who knows the joys and challenges of ministry and who is trained to listen to the questions, rather than giving answers. This is the role of a trained mentor.

Mentors

Mentors are guides walking alongside us in the learning process, with the experience of knowing the navigation points ahead. Once a course is navigated several times, the ability to spot changes in conditions, adjust, innovate in response to the unexpected, and pause to assess shifting dynamics becomes more intuitive. A mentor can share that perspective with the new priest as they navigate this course.

At the outset, it is essential to clarify what a mentor is not. A mentor does not pour his or her stories of ministry into the head of the priest and expect that to be sufficient information to work out strategic next steps. That is the pedagogical model of the expert imparting information.

In addition, a mentor is not a coach, spiritual director, or therapist. These areas of a spiritual leader's life will naturally arise in mentoring conversations. A mentor is aware when additional professional support is needed.

A mentor is an experienced spiritual leader, usually a clergyperson, who serves for the benefit of the individual and the learning community's learning and growth. A mentor listens deeply and asks good questions that arise from the accumulated wisdom of ministry practice. A strong mentor keeps their own experience in the background and speaks to support the clergyperson as they put together the dynamics of the current experience and context to identify potential next steps. Then, the mentor offers a structured conversation to prioritize these steps. The mentor also provides a structure for accountability. "When are you going to complete this step, and when are you going to get back to me?" is a common question, creating a timeline for action and a check-in soon afterward.

Just as the peer learning community can be a standard bearer for best practices in ministry, so can the mentor. Over the years, some of the questions I have heard are:

- "Can a husband and wife sit on a vestry at the same time?"
- "I am in a small parish with not much money. Does the parish need to conduct an audit on the financial records?"
- "The treasurer is the only counter for the collection on Sunday. What do I do?"
- "Someone filed a complaint about me to the bishop. What do I do now?"
- "Can I pay for that out of my discretionary fund?"

- "The former rector is attending worship. Is that allowed?"
- "I am exhausted. I can't seem to take time off."

Some of these questions have specific actionable answers. For example: "The treasurer cannot be the only Sunday counter, so let's see a practical step you can take as soon as possible to change the situation." The last question, which is more of a statement of despair, demands a different kind of answer. While the mentor can explain the importance of self-care, they also need to know that self-care and arranging to rest are two different things. The mentor can explore why the priest cannot take time off. Is this a mentoring issue, a therapeutic concern, or a time-management challenge? Could it reflect a deeper insight into the priest's personal circumstances? There may be family pressures, or it may simply be the aftermath of an especially demanding period in the life of the parish or the priest. A mentor can help explore these possibilities.

Or it could be due to obvious stress. I heard "I am exhausted, I can't take time off" frequently during the COVID-19 pandemic. Many priests experienced the same anxiety and trauma when both family members and parish members died. Listening to these priests reminded me of the AIDS epidemic in the late 1980s. One priest told me he was leaving the ministry after presiding over twenty funerals of friends in just four months. During the COVID-19 shutdown, the anxiety, the uncertainty, the loss of community and connection, reinventing worship and pastoral care, the deaths, and the funerals exhausted clergy. Yet many parishioners assumed, like so many other tragedies, that the priests could handle it because they are "spiritual people."

Many priests carried the load and found ways to cope. I was impressed by one priest who said straightforwardly to his vestry, "I am exhausted. I need two weeks off." This was not in lieu of his regular time off. This was additional time off. Many priests spent valuable time in peer groups discussing parish needs and their own. Mentors helped guide the discussions deeper. (I heard these examples from 2019 to 2021 when I was directing the Thriving in Ministry program.) When standards are developed in a crisis, like COVID-19, priests described the mentor and peer group as a "lifeline."

We get a more complex, nuanced question when we return to the grieving son I discussed earlier. A priest asks her mentor and peer learning group, "I am still caring for the son consumed by grief over the death of his mother. It's been more than a year. His family is turning to me for help. The son is stuck. What do I do?" This question, in the context of both colleagues who know her and a mentor who knows her, is heartfelt, pastoral, theological, and personal, requires professional skill, and is a learning reflection for everyone, including the mentor. There is no one perfect answer, while there are several potential answers for this priest, this family, this grieving son. If a harmful mistake has been made, the mentor can suggest possible repairs. If the mentor senses a place where the priest cannot move forward, then privately or in the next mentoring conversation, the mentor can bring up the topic to suggest therapy.

A participant in a peer learning community may prefer to discuss some questions one-on-one with the mentor before presenting them to the group. Sometimes the group will not know the answer. This is where participants can benefit from a mentor's experience in ministry. The mentor can break down the components of the question and suggest possible answers. The mentor then helps the group put together potential answers. Sometimes the answer is a clear *no* even if some peers in the group prefer to accommodate personalities in the parish with a squishy *maybe*. The mentor can guide the group toward the best practice while addressing the discomfort of group participants.

A mentor is also a reflective practitioner. From the experience of reflective practice over years of ministry, a mentor offers a long view of ministry while honoring the present moment. Especially for a new priest, vocational formation takes place in the present moment, with each new piece of information and each act of support. A mentor may also notice and identify a pattern in a new priest that is not serving that priest well. Why keep tripping over the same unnoticed rock? A mentor may counsel patience in interpersonal communication or counsel contacting the appropriate persons if misconduct has occurred.

It is not unusual for new priests assigned to parishes as priests-in-charge to discover layers of financial practices that make sense to the treasurer but do not meet the test of sound financial management. It is also not unusual for a new priest to discover a history of parish communication controlled by one person or family to the degree that the entire parish remains stuck. A new priest may quickly notice unhealthy or unhelpful parish dynamics because, in the early stages of ministry, they have little experience navigating or accommodating such patterns. This can lead them to focus too intensely on correcting what is wrong rather than discerning which changes are truly necessary. A mentor can help the new priest pace the rate of change and approach the work with greater balance and perspective. These examples are a handful of what a mentor could offer any priest, and especially a new priest.

All mentoring conversations can combine these characteristics about history, parish dynamics, working with perspective as well as providing support. A mentoring conversation skillfully incorporates elements that encourage the mentee to go deeper, reflect on the experience, and take a new action.

Other important roles in formation that are *not* for the mentor were briefly mentioned earlier in this chapter: a mentor is not a therapist. A mentor is not a coach. A mentor is not a spiritual director. A mentor is not making a decision on behalf of the priest. And as mentioned earlier, the mentor is not an expert pouring all his success stories into the priest. At times, the mentor's comments may be close to those of a therapist, a spiritual director, a directive, or a personal story about ministry. The mentor can suggest that the priest speak to their therapist or spiritual director about a specific question. However, the mentoring relationship is not directed primarily toward therapy, spiritual direction, making decisions for the priest, or sharing expertise.

Mentoring as a Ministry

Mentoring as a ministry is an intentional, guided conversation shaped by a priest's depth of experience in ministry practice, offered for the benefit of the clergy mentee and the church. Clergy with more than fifteen years of service often feel a natural desire to share the wisdom they have gained over the years. This becomes even more common as a clergy person prepares to retire. In my experience, clergy want to be generative and creative. And, often upon learning about intentional support for new clergy or for a stage of ministry, experienced clergy often say, "I wish I had that! How can I be a part of this?"

Yet not every clergy person is a natural mentor. We all have mixed motivations. The key phrase, here, is "for the benefit of whom." Mentoring as a ministry is not about the mentor. The ministry of mentoring is focused outward toward the mentee and the church. Of course, as mentoring unfolds, the mentor learns about themselves, discovers their own inner work to grow as a mentor, and practices with proven mentoring tools. The mentor's growth is an intended secondary benefit. However, if the mentor engages in this ministry primarily for self-improvement, that motivation will be painfully obvious to the mentee, leading to a lack of trust and the disintegration of the mentoring relationship. The ministry of a mentor acting "for the benefit of" is about forming a trusting relationship so that the deeper mentoring conversations take place.

Mentoring is also about conversations. I call these intentional mentoring conversations because they are not casual small talk about life in the parish. Instead, the mentor and the mentee are familiar with the basic framework of a conversation designed to take them deeper. Earlier, I referred to the opening sentence of that conversation: "What is the most important part of your life or ministry we need to be talking about today?" Ideally, the mentee is prepared to answer that question when the mentoring conversation begins. The mentor can also guide the mentee to sort out issues that feel like competing priorities.

Susan Scott, in *Fierce Conversations,* says, "The conversation is the relationship."[1] In other words, if you are not talking about it, "it" is not part of your relationship. The relationship is only as deep as the conversation you are willing to engage in. When important and impactful

1. Susan Scott, *Fierce Conversations* (Berkley, 2004).

parts are left out of the conversation, the relationship is less than it could be. The mentor is less effective. The mentee learns less. And mentors and mentees miss the opportunity to engage in life-changing conversations and long-lasting relationships.

Experienced clergy and those seeking guidance can come together in a variety of ways. Sometimes the relationship forms organically as the two priests work together in a parish or on a shared project. In other cases, the mentoring relationship may be formalized through an intentional agreement to work together. It may also remain informal, developing naturally through ongoing conversations within their common ministry.

Another way is for a less experienced clergy person to seek out conversations with a more experienced person. Usually, the clergy seeking to learn is drawn to the more experienced person through personality, interest in a specific ministry (e.g., social justice), aspiration for a possible future (e.g., a large parish), or a focus on an area of ministry practice (e.g., preaching). The mentee initiates the mentorship, and the mentor agrees to the relationship. The specific request for a mentoring relationship opens the possibility of scheduling meetings, focusing on the mentee's questions, holding each other accountable for actions tested and taken, and using mentoring resources to enhance the conversation. These mentoring relationships can be lifelong.

Yet another way is through a formal program that offers a mentoring process for a specific stage of ministry. Examples include the Virtual Curacy program at Berkeley Divinity School (BDS) at Yale and the Launching into Ministry program at Virginia Theological Seminary (VTS). Graduating seniors and new clergy are invited to apply or participate in a two-year program with an experienced, trained mentor. The seminaries recruit and train mentors so that mentoring conversations share a common foundation and set of tools. While some consider the program and ask how they will be "matched" with a mentor, "matching" is different from organically meeting a mentor or intentionally seeking out a specific mentor. The matching focus on shared experience is similar across contexts, e.g., rebuilding a parish, regions of the country (e.g., Colorado vs. Vermont), and the age of the participant (e.g., a second-career priest). The mentoring relationship usually continues throughout the program.

In all these examples, the experienced clergy person and the mentee learn together for the benefit of the mentee and the church. The mentor draws on her experience in ministry practice as a foundation for listening deeply and guiding wisely.

Mentoring is a three-in-one ministry that encompasses pastoral care, leadership development, and vocational formation.

On the pastoral side, the mentor serves as a shepherd leading the mentee to places of safety and substance. The mentor remains attentive for warning signs and helps chart steady and trustworthy paths. Mentoring, like all solid pastoral relationships, upholds clear boundaries, respects the mentee's autonomy, and keeps confidential information strictly confidential.

Mentoring as a ministry is also a form of leadership development. Priests with experience as spiritual leaders in a parish bring vision and clarity, both vocationally and personally. This honing of the person and skills within the vocation of the priesthood is an example for a colleague with less experience. The colleague (mentee) can observe and hear how the mentor integrates information, treats people, reflects, and clearly communicates. These are all qualities of a leader. Then, in mentoring conversations, the colleague practices identifying priorities, developing a strategy, reflecting on experience, conducting self-assessment, seeking out new information, and other multifaceted aspects of ministry. These are all skills of a leader. The mentee, through both mentoring conversations and the mentor's example in ministry, observes, practices, and learns ways to lead in their own context.

Lastly, mentoring as a ministry is for vocational development. Here is the dimension of mentoring that includes the priest's spiritual practices, discernment of God's guidance, self-awareness, and professional growth. The mentor guides the mentee to honor the sacred call to serve as a friend of Christ and, at the same time, not to take themselves too seriously! While a mentor is not a spiritual director, therapist, life coach, or professor, these roles overlap in mentoring for vocational development. Formation experiences that occur before serving in a parish include academic study, prayer life, spiritual direction, and, sometimes, therapy. Vocational development moves deeper into the individual's personal and professional identity as they serve in a parish, live as a priest in a parish, in their household, and in public. The mentor brings knowledge and experience from his or her own vital personal prayer life, from a discipline of self-reflection, and ongoing practices that enhance the multiple skills for ministry.

The emphasis is not on any one of these dimensions over another, but rather on integrating them into a way of life shaped by a call from God. Here, mentoring is unquestionably theological. Mentoring is translating a priest's daily activities into the theological meaning of *call.* Mentoring can also be translating the daily activities/professional skills/spiritual passions into the theological meaning of lay leadership. By offering a small incident for reflection that could connect to the creation of the universe, mentoring is about guiding us to discover the extraordinary in the ordinary.

Throughout, I describe mentoring as a ministry that is pastoral, developmental, especially for leadership, and vocational growth. A mentor, through years of experience, integrates these three essential areas of being a priest into their life. As a mentoring ministry unfolds, the mentor's foundation in the essentials informs, guides, teaches, and supports the mentee in integrating her experience and growing in her call to be a friend of Christ.

The characteristics of an effective mentor are woven into examples of what mentors do within a learning community. It may be helpful to summarize these qualities: an experienced priest drawn to mentoring for the benefit of both the mentee and the church; a commitment to continuous learning grounded in reflective practice; a disciplined spiritual life shaped by prayer, worship, retreats, and self-care; an engaged learner and attentive listener; and, ultimately, a reflective practitioner.

The three clergy at the beginning of the chapter intentionally continued their friendship as a learning relationship. Through shared experience, they learned about ministry and about themselves for the benefit of one another and the church. This marks the beginning of a mentoring relationship, promising to celebrate the joy of ministry and to offer support for smooth sailing during choppy seas.

Coaching

Almost always after speaking about mentors, the question comes up, "What about coaching?" There are several distinctions between the mentors and coaches. I define a mentor as a priest with demonstrated experience in the practice of ministry who asks good questions and offers informed guidance to the mentee from his or her deep wisdom of ministry practice. The mentor knows the nuances of the profession and of the vocation of ministry. The mentor has the long view through experience.

A good coach asks insightful questions, empowering the client to discover their own solutions and next steps. A coach may or may not have experience in the practice. A mentor also asks good questions, sometimes the same as the coach. It is the long, tested experience in the practice that gives the mentor the nuanced knowledge gained through years of reflective practice.

Another distinction is that a mentoring relationship is intentionally tailored to the stage of growth, while a coaching relationship focuses more narrowly on an issue, question, or problem. In my definition, mentoring is more open and holistic, while coaching is shorter-term and goal-focused. For example, a clergy coach may work with a new priest on relationships with the vestry and set a goal for ten coaching sessions. A mentor would plan to work with the mentee for two years, focusing on the priest's stage of ministry and the characteristic changes that are key to that stage. For newer priests, that includes developing relationships with lay leaders and skills in governance. While not everyone agrees with my definitions, I find it helpful to differentiate each role.

Each role has a specific intention. A priest may need a coach to focus on a specific issue she needs to work through now. However, if the issue is not sufficiently resolved at the end of the contract, again, let's say ten sessions, then the contract can be extended with a new stated focus and time, or perhaps there is a decision to call a consultant.

Alternatively, a priest may also begin ministry in a new parish with the support of a mentor. Entering well—learning the parish's history, communication patterns, and unspoken expectations—offers rich opportunities for early conversations. Topics such as loneliness, the practical "how-to" of new responsibilities, family transitions, and the presence of informal leaders all shape the priest's leadership. A mentor typically raises these questions proactively. A coach, by contrast, may arrive at more personal issues only as they naturally become part of the coaching focus.

In practice, it can be difficult to distinguish between a coach and a mentor. An especially adept coach may say to a client as the conversation explores vocational future, "Let me put on my mentor hat so that I am listening and speaking with you toward a bigger picture." Or, in a mentoring conversation that gets stuck on an issue, an experienced mentor may say, "Let me put on my coach hat so I can ask questions to help you drill down on that issue."

Mentoring follows a pattern of questions intended to develop Clarity; however, good mentoring does not stop with Clarity about one subject. A mentor may ask for further reflection on areas of pastoral care, self-care, family dynamics, and on how this process is supporting the

Peers

Intentional mutual learning also happens in peer learning communities. The three seminarians/new priests in the narrative at the beginning of the chapter formed an informal peer-learning community out of necessity. In the absence of others to reflect on their experience, they benefited from the conversations they had with one another.

For example, during the initial six months of ministry, the priests discussed the "firsts": the first baptism, the first wedding, the first funeral of a respected parish member, the first time handling the day-to-day responsibilities while the rector was on vacation, and the first vestry meeting. They shared the clash of confidence and competence in a "first." "Of course I can do a funeral, how many times have I been over it, it will be fine . . . and this is my first one solo!" Learning that each of them experienced the simultaneous feelings of being ready and anxious affirmed that they were not alone. The conversation opened to explore other places that loneliness creeps in, ways to cope, and ways to accept. And the conversation strengthened their support for one another.

Peers are significant partners in formation because they share a common experience. When the going gets rough, when experiences are uncomfortable, when growth seems stuck, and when nothing seems to work, we all tend to assume we are alone. No one can possibly share our experience. Peer group members "normalize" both the rough times and the joyful times because they share the same experiences. This is especially true during times of transition—whether entering a new ministry or parish, navigating a shifting life stage, or experiencing loss. In such moments, we reshape our sense of self because the world around us has changed. After the death of a spouse, for example, the work of grief becomes a process of literally reconstructing one's identity.

When we move to a new call, we transition all our daily life activities to new people and places. Peers through shared experience reassure one another that we are not alone.

The feeling of isolation is especially powerful for new clergy, who are moving from a close-knit community of worship and academic study to the diffuse life of a parish and a diocese. Impromptu theological conversations are no longer possible. Discussion of next Sunday's sermon needs to be intentionally scheduled rather than spontaneously happen at the lunch table. Reflecting on Sunday morning unfolds in your own head rather than on the way to class Monday morning. Many of the daily interactions that clergy experience during their time in the academy no longer happen. Add to that the weekly planning and preparation, and professional interaction must now happen when the priest is alone.

The vocation of a priest does feel isolating. Peers and peer learning communities can create another form of daily, weekly, and monthly theological conversations, sermon preparation, and reflection on parish experiences.

The common bond is most often found around a shared stage of ministry practice, as there is a wider range of shared experiences. (In the previous chapter, The stages of ministry describes the range of these collective experiences.)

And peer groups can also be formed around a ministry practice of common interest. One example is church planters. Another example is clergy in parishes with schools. One diocese offered self-care clergy peer groups based on various areas of interest and spiritual renewal, such as fly fishing, cycling, and chess.

As we have seen, some peer learning communities are intentionally formed to focus on a specific stage of ministry, such as the Initial Years of Ministry. Other peer learning communities may form for the specific task of developing skills for a more complex leadership role, such as seeking executive leadership, or a particular dynamic in ministry, such as clergy couples serving in the same parish. A peer learning community is designed to focus on a specific practice of ministry in the current context of the participant, with questions based on recent experience.

For instance, clergy couples may discuss the impact of gender differences and how each couple addresses that challenge publicly with the parish. A communication challenge with a husband-and-wife clergy couple is that parishioners assume the husband is in charge. Yet, in some instances, the wife is the rector, and the husband is the associate with another vocation, such as teaching or serving as a chaplain. One couple uses a set of consistent, short messages that clarify each spouse's role, indicate who is responsible for a given ministry, or remind parish members that any message intended for the other spouse must be delivered by the parishioner directly. There can be no "Please tell your wife (husband) for me." After a while, other members use these short, informative phrases to smooth the distinction between the priests. This couple found that the informal method of setting the standard and then allowing the message to gradually spread among the community worked. A parish with a different communication style would need a different communication pathway.

The learning emerges from the distinct ways each couple vocationally navigates the impact of gender differences in their priestly roles. Support takes shape through conversations that surface finer points and nuances—both for the couple and for the parish context. These dialogues clarify the underlying dynamics and create a foundation for forming an effective response.

Peer learning communities differ from support groups. Support groups tend to focus primarily on personal perspectives and as a space to share perspectives that a clergy person wishes to keep private. In the example of clergy couples, a support group would likely discuss the personal challenges of being a clergy couple in the same parish, how gender differences in their public ministry impact their marriage, what they consider private about their conversations, how they handle the inevitable curiosity of parishioners, and address the inevitable triangulation between each spouse and the parish. The support focuses on each couple and how to meet the challenges they would not discuss with others.

The peer learning community adds another dimension. The personal perspective in ministry is an essential part of reflecting on any challenge. Generating new, abstract ideas for addressing that challenge naturally brings into the conversation the wider context of the parish—its history, its patterns through a family-systems lens, behaviors related to authority and gender differences, communication styles, and the character of the surrounding community. In this way, the peer learning community provides not only personal support and growth but also a space to engage the evolving conditions of ministry practice and navigate the unknown with greater awareness.

While it might seem easy to merge the purposes of a peer learning community and a support group, the two groups are distinct. The purpose of a support group is to support one another. This usually means careful and compassionate listening to the issues each member of the group shares. Support is essential in the life of ministry. However, support may or may not mean processing the issue or looking for different approaches. Without an intentional process, support groups can be each person's list of hassles and woes. Then, the support is agreeing on how awful the situation really is.

In a peer learning community, there is an intentional process to listen carefully and compassionately so that the conversation generates new perspectives, new potential actions, and new learning. Support arises from this process as an intended secondary purpose.

Peer learning communities also explore and reflect on specific challenges in ministry practice. One peer presents a recent experience in ministry practice generated by question prompts shared by all participants in the group. The presenter shares her perspective, the challenge and question, and then asks for specific help from her peers.

Along with the challenge offered by the presenting participant, the other members of the peer learning community may also offer challenges to their colleague. These challenges are not criticisms. Instead, they serve as gentle reminders of the best practices in ministry.

A challenge might involve wondering whether a colleague is becoming too close to a member of the congregation and may be crossing a personal boundary. It could be a direct comment about an overloaded schedule—insight offered from a peer who can see the situation more clearly. A challenge may begin with "Have you considered . . . ?" to introduce an alternative perspective. It can also take the form of noticing an absence, such as, "I'm wondering why I'm not hearing anything about . . ."

The support and challenge take place within the consistent structure of a peer learning community. Each community sets a regular meeting time and publishes an agenda in advance. Each meeting also includes a check-in, accountability for actions taken from the decisions made in prior meetings, and a reflective practice presented by a member of the group. In addition, there are opening and closing times designated for prayer, silence, scripture reading, or other acts of devotion. The mentor/coach arranges the logistics for the meeting, publishes the agenda, and guides the group. In those peer groups that do not have a mentor, one group member serves as the coordinator for meeting logistics and agenda. The presenter's role in each session rotates among the members.

Learning Goals

Each member of the peer learning community identifies learning goals. The goals that are typically for personal development/vocational often include acquiring new information to develop a capacity for ministry or honing a skill. For example, a priest in the Initial Years of Ministry may have personal learning goals in time management, a ministry goal focused on stewardship, and a ministry skill focused on improving preaching. The goals are usually formed in one-to-one conversations with the mentor. Also, in that discussion, the participant and mentor break down each goal into the steps needed to accomplish it, a time frame, the resources needed, and a description of what success looks like.

Brené Brown, the well-known writer, professor, and social researcher, uses the expression "Paint Done" with her team. Paint Done is the picture of what the supervisor of the action envisions for a completed job. If the supervisor is not painting a clear picture, the team member can verbally paint a picture of "Done" to test if that picture shows the goal completed.[2] When both parties agree that the hypothetical picture is complete, then the task can be launched.

The learning goals may be written on a chart developed by my company, Soul Assets, for this purpose. Some peer learning communities share their charts with one another. Some dedicate one meeting to share their learning goals. At each subsequent meeting, time is set aside, and the participant is accountable to their peers for describing movement/learning toward the goal.

Accountability

Accountability to one another in the group is evident in both participants' conduct and discussions. The peer learning group reviews a basic covenant for meetings, which includes confidentiality and a commitment to attend all meetings. The group may add other norms to the covenant. They are accountable to one another for keeping those commitments. In discussions, participants

2. Brené Brown, *Dare to Lead: Brave Work. Tough Conversations. Whole Hearts.* (Random House, 2018), 44.

demonstrate accountability by sharing their learning goals at each stage of development, actively participating in reflective practice, and investing in one another's learning. Participants get out of the group what they put in. When a member is not committed or not interested in their own learning, the other participants can tell.

The participants are also accountable to their mentors. Mentors should meet monthly with each participant one-to-one, usually for an hour. (In personal learning communities of eight to ten, it is usual for two mentors to shepherd the group.) During one-to-one meetings with the mentor, the conversation may begin with learning goals and delve into the obstacles the participant is discovering. Are those obstacles personal, relational, or systemic in the parish? Or the conversation may start with a classic coaching question: "What is the most important thing we need to be talking about today?" The participant is responsible for his or her own learning by honestly and candidly discussing what is happening. The participant can use this deeper discussion to work through the stickier issues and then bring those back to the next peer learning community with either this insight or how that insight helped her move forward.

Growing Pastoral Identity

As the context and members of parish ministry change rapidly, it becomes harder to repeat the same year of ministry twice. There was a time when parishioners could tell which Liturgical Year they were in from the sermon, because over time the priest had worked out all the sermons and repeated them in a cycle.

Now, parish members and clergy move to new churches much more frequently. The average stay of a priest in one parish is four years. Some churches are still recovering from the COVID-19 pandemic. Some are facing shifts in the surrounding community beyond their control, and which inevitably impact the parish. These shifting dynamics of parish life mean that formation in ministry means learning the needs and expectations of each new parish. Increasingly, clergy in the initial years begin ministry as a clergy-in-charge, serving the congregation for a contracted period, such as three years. As a new clergy member, they experience the "firsts" of ministry, including all the personal changes that come after seminary, the new information of a parish, and the new relationships that come with it, all simultaneously. It is not easy to set aside what feels like personal time for reflection when the needs of running a parish for the first time are also a very demanding experience.

Growing pastoral identity means learning who you are as a priest-pastor-teacher-leader. Reflecting on ministry as a continual method to grow and to learn from yields a deeper sense of pastoral identity for that priest. Priests come to understand their identity through the ministry they practice and within the particular communities they serve. Yet in seasons of sustained turmoil—when time for intentional reflection is scarce, and the focus shifts to simple survival—spiritual leaders tend to rely only on what they already know. As a result, their capacity to grow, adapt, and respond to new situations and challenges is limited.

Pastoral identity also changes when a priest moves from one stage of ministry to another. A priest in the first year of ministry is not the same as a priest with seven years of experience. Pastoral identity develops through the practice of ministry, revealing new dimensions of who you are. It takes shape when a challenge you doubted you could navigate reaches a safe landing place. At other times, pastoral identity is forged when a misstep grows into an unexpected storm. It also deepens as the clergyperson strengthens core skills in pastoral care, preaching, teaching, and administration.

The same is true of a priest with fifteen years of experience seeking skills in executive leadership because he feels called to a more complex ministry. Pastoral identity grows through steady, positive shifts—small increments that, over the course of the year, ensure the clergyperson is not the same priest she was when the year began.

Sadly, the same can be true of negative changes in pastoral identity. A priest's pastoral identity forms regardless of whether the experience benefits or harms them. Negative changes can lead to clergy leaving the ministry entirely after five years. Negative changes among priests can also lead to distrust, strained relationships, and little energy for the vocation. This is especially dangerous when priests in the Initial Years of Ministry become priests-in-charge of a parish with no support from an experienced mentor or coach. The new priest doesn't yet know what she doesn't know. The consequences—otherwise avoidable—often become painful mistakes for both the priest and the parish, with effects that can shape ministry for years to come.

Ideally, a healthy pastoral identity is *wise*, *kind*, *balanced*, and *curious*. *Wisdom* is created by the priest as each year of ministry practice unfolds, and reflective practice on ministry creates new knowledge from that experience. Wisdom is many things. It is restrained and clear speech. It is a sense of timing. It is a learned or intuitive reading of human beings by their actions, not by what they say. Wisdom lies in knowing when a conflict must be addressed immediately and when allowing it to simmer will be beneficial. In other words, wisdom is learning which fires to put out and when. Wisdom is learning to be patient even when you think you are straining beyond your ability. Wisdom is about learning patience, but it is also about acting quickly when necessary. Wisdom is starting the conversations everyone else thinks should happen, and no one else will start.

Being *kind* changes the world. Being kind does not mean always accommodating, or avoiding conflict, or being able to make a joke in a tense exchange. Brené Brown says, "clear is kind."[3] It is possible to be kind when

3. Brown, *Dare to Lead*, 44.

handling conflict because, as the leader, you worked to be clear about the needs of the situation. Thus, kind is clear, and kind is open. Kind recognizes at the same time the integrity of yourself and of others. Kindness is always welcome. As human beings, we each carry our own strengths and our struggles. A wise mentor once told me, "You never know what people are bringing with them into the pews."

Is parish ministry the priest's only interest? If so, that is not a healthy *balance*. Balance means having at least one interest that connects you with people outside the church—a kind of personal hinterland. It also means practicing self-care and recognizing that caring for yourself is not selfish. Balance involves setting appropriate boundaries for the parish, especially around family, particularly if there are small children. Balance is planning for a colleague to cover funerals while on vacation or on sabbatical so that you do not need to return, and helping the parish set their expectations around those events.

I recall a conversation with a parish member during a time shortly before Easter when the parish experienced nine deaths, all long-time members. It seemed that every day, funeral directors, usher teams, altar guild members, bereavement reception volunteers, and musicians were at the church, caring for the families. I said to one of the ushers after the ninth funeral, with Holy Week so close, "I worry about all the other things that we did not get done." He kindly said to me, "We know that this is what you were supposed to be doing." Our lay leaders can remind us of the importance of balance. His comment gave me permission to reschedule some commitments so I could recover and prepare for the week ahead. Balance also means embracing multiple roles—priest, mother, spouse, book lover, horseback rider, and even someone who delights in searching for frogs in puddles.

In the early years of ministry, when wisdom born of reflection is still forming, a healthy *curiosity* will help smooth out the bumps. Curiosity is being alert for new observations. Curiosity is knowing there are things about ministry practice that you don't know. Curiosity is asking for what you need. Do you want to practice doing a baptism? Ask a knowledgeable clergy colleague to walk you through the liturgy and then observe your practice. Curiosity is asking someone you trust for feedback. Curiosity involves observing experienced clergy, learning from their experiences, and understanding what to do and what not to do. Curiosity is balancing two or more opinions that are in tension with one another, and knowing you can also maintain your opinion. Curiosity is knowing it is not necessary to decide everything right now, and asking: "What else might be needed?"

Learning Congregations

A learning congregation serves as the third key partner in the cycle of adult learning for a spiritual leader. Such congregations intentionally embrace practices that support the priest's ministry and ongoing formation. As noted earlier, this formation unfolds through the lived experience of the clergy person.

The formation can be positive, offering opportunities for reflection with mentors and peers and pathways to develop a pastoral identity. Positive formation enriches one's ministry. Or formation can be negative, characterized by chaos, disruption, and ongoing conflict that leaves little time for reflection and growth. Negative formation can drain ministry. A learning congregation creates the conditions for priests to succeed.

I am most familiar with learning congregations for clergy in the first five years of ministry. In those congregations, forming new clergy is the congregation's ministry responsibility as much as it is the clergy of the parish who are involved as mentor(s). Clear, consistent communication prior to the arrival of new clergy helps prepare the congregation to understand the purpose of this ministry of formation. Financial costs to the congregation are stated and repeated. (Nothing is free, even if having a new clergy person can be called "free help.") The impact on the current clergy's time is assessed. The tenure of the new clergy person is stated so that the congregation understands that they are helping to form a priest who will ultimately be sent forth to serve the wider church.

Opportunities for congregation members to join committees, take on tasks, and engage with conversation starters are clearly communicated and regularly reinforced. The purpose is to bring as many people as possible into the outermost ring of the information circle as possible before the new clergy person arrives. Thus, forming a priest in a healthy congregational context is a ministry of the congregation.

A characteristic of a healthy learning congregation is that it provides a safe environment for learning. First, a learning congregation should expect to try new ideas and also expect mistakes. Mistakes are only mistakes if there is no learning. Mistakes are also not a time to try to dismiss discomfort with a joke and minimize the event. Second, a learning congregation needs to spread good news about the new clergy person. Parish members are always curious about their priests. (Priests are also always curious about their parishioners.) Rather than guessing, share information that is complementary, and that, as the speaker, you know is true.

Many learning congregations establish support teams. Members of the congregation are invited to join. The support team members, including the spiritual leader, receive training from me, and with Soul Assets Consulting tools and processes, they will use over the next two years. Meeting once a month, the team provides a forum where the clergyperson or spiritual leader can ask questions, reflect on their experience, and receive constructive feedback.

In the case of a priest in the initial years of ministry or of a priest new to a congregation, it is an opportunity for the clergy person to learn more about the history, the surrounding area, the challenges, and the celebrations directly from parish members. It is also a time for these parishioners to come to know the clergy person as a whole person. It is also important for clergy to understand how they are perceived by others. Offering this feedback appropriately, especially in the initial years, is a gift to clergy. Rather than focusing primarily on the transition into a new congregation, the support team focuses on creating the conditions for success for both the spiritual leader and the parish. For a priest in the Initial Years of Ministry, the support team addresses characteristics of that stage of ministry.

Members of the support team are also trained in appropriate feedback. Unlike the one-sided feedback from a superior, support team members learn what I call dialogue feedback. The priest is asked to describe what she likes about a particular area of ministry, for example, teaching. Using a recent teaching example, she first describes what went well for her. Then she describes what she did not like about her teaching, what she might change. Usually, a time limit of five to ten minutes is set for the clergy person's part of the dialogue.

Part of being a support team member involves being present as the spiritual leader leads the congregation. This engaged presence opens the dialogue for the second part of the feedback process. The members describe their experience of how things went. They are trained to give specific examples, such as clarity of delivery, use of media, offering of resource materials, and whether they could hear the speaker. They are asked to share their experience of the priest's energy and commitment to the topic. Then the dialogue moves to what could be improved. Slow down the pace? Speed it up? Take fewer questions? Leave time for more questions? Practice managing the dynamics in the room. These are a handful of specific areas that might be mentioned.

During Soul Assets training, support team members are also advised that if an observation feels too personal or seems far outside the priest's awareness, they may bring the concern to the team chair and/or the mentor instead of raising it directly. Chances are that others notice that same tender spot and wonder how to bring it up. What is important is that appropriate, honest feedback for learning is offered.

Mentors, as noted earlier, are also part of the constellation that shapes a learning congregation. Their role as guides provides leaders with a framework, thoughtful questions, and, when necessary, new information to help navigate toward the intended point on the horizon. In a learning congregation, a mentor may come from within the community or from another parish.

Just as in sailing, adjusting to the dynamic, ever-changing conditions of ministry requires reflective practice on ministry experiences, intentional learning with peers, and ideally a learning congregation. With this foundation, self-directed spiritual leaders can create continuous learning and conversations. However, it is challenging for a self-directed leader to create, maintain, and nourish this full process of reflective practice without outside expertise.

Returning to chapter 1, leadership development requires partners in order to generate full reflective practice opportunities. Spiritual leaders whose ministry is mentoring are the first group prepared to form mentoring conversations with individuals, groups, and congregations. Leaders who are well-trained, act with integrity, and operate independently of any single diocesan structure are best positioned to meet participants' needs. When participants join peer learning communities across dioceses, the conversations reveal that many questions are common to the stage in ministry and are often not entirely due to regional factors, the diocesan bishop, local lay leadership, or the short-sightedness of one priest.

When creating reflective practice opportunities from within a diocese that draw participants from within that same diocese, extremely high standards of confidentiality are essential. Especially for clergy in the initial years who find themselves vulnerable to the opinions of others, solid assurance that their questions and mistakes remain with the mentor and within the group is the crucial ingredient in starting a group. Otherwise, trust will erode, and the group will be unable to navigate changing conditions.

Spiritual leaders in the ministry of coaching can also offer reflective practice opportunities. However, in my mind, in such a situation, the coach is becoming more of a mentor because the conversations are longer-term and often move beyond skill-based practice.

The best possible scenario is a small fleet of mentors trained to offer full reflective practice opportunities so that, as a clergy person is ready to opt into a group, a potential practice group is also ready. Being ready may mean stepping into a storm or into a new stage of ministry. A new form of Reflective Learning—rooted in the lived practice of ministry—lies on the horizon for those who, from this shore, look toward the point of sail.

A common time when clergy step into a storm or a new stage of ministry is graduation from seminary with a new call to a new parish. Everything the clergy person learned in seminary is a foundation, and everything ahead is looking to a new point of sail. The next chapter explores ways to integrate academic learning with reflective practice.

CHAPTER 6

Theological Education and Reflective Practice

I never learned that in seminary.

—Anonymous quote by a multitude of priests

A familiar saying among theologically trained spiritual leaders is "I never learned that in seminary!" Over the years, I observed two reactions to this remark. Anyone associated with a seminary, especially faculty, is offended. The remark implies that academic training missed something vital, something obvious that a spiritual leader should be taught. The remark also makes the judgment that the seminary failed to fulfill its mission to train priests and spiritual leaders for ministry in the church.

The other reaction is the eyeroll among other spiritual leaders. "Yeah, I know what you mean! I learned so much on my own" is the implied and sometimes a not-so-silent remark. It is as if theological education has done little to prepare them for the realities of ministry practice.

Yet the seminaries did not fail, and spiritual leaders only fully learn the practice of ministry when they are completely immersed in it. *Each place of learning is appropriate for that particular stage of ministry development.*

In a seminary, the spiritual leader is a student. The academic learning process is designed to present abundant, complex information from studied, accomplished, experienced, and informed faculty in an orderly manner, allowing students to build a knowledge base. Much of the information is new to a seminary student. The student is presented with many new concepts. Academic learning is the process by which new ideas challenge long-held beliefs. New ideas shift perspectives. The classroom, the lunchroom, the walk to class, and informal conversations are all times when students intellectually work through these ideas.

And much of this emerging knowledge base is interwoven with related disciplines—linking theology with philosophy, Biblical studies with the history of interpretation, ethics with historical contexts (often shaped by the theological influences of particular denominations or countries of origin), and church history with world history, whether Western-focused or expanded to include the global church. Can one study biblical interpretation without understanding biblical literalism and its social, historical, and political impact? Can one study ethics without learning about Roman Catholic social teaching, the Hebrew prophets, or Dietrich Bonhoeffer?

As this new foundation of knowledge is forming, the student also learns the disciplines of pastoring that, at a minimum, require knowledge of the bible and of theology.

Preaching is taught in a seminary. It is a discipline that a spiritual leader will engage in almost every week. Pastoral care is also taught in seminaries and through programs like Clinical Pastoral Education. Theological knowledge of the human condition, a theology of hope, the process of grieving, the effects of trauma, and the cycle of addiction are all rooted in what has been called "care of the human soul." Preaching and pastoral care are two examples of classes taught in seminary that directly carry over into ministry. They are also two examples that depend on the foundation of knowledge learned in academic study.

Academic study is the foundation of a spiritual leader's information system. You might say it is the basic navigation system of the ship. When the journey's parameters are entered into the navigation system, the system plots the corresponding coordinates. Imagine that the present moment—the person's situation and the priest's care—is "entered" into a theological navigation system during a pastoral call or conversation. The system would then offer the priest coordinates for navigating the moment, and also coordinates to help this person.

In the initial stage of ministry, the spiritual leader may find the system slow to process. With practice, i.e., experience, the complex workings of the navigation system flow more easily. This may be an oversimplified image; however, an important dimension of spiritual leadership is to think theologically with and on behalf of those in one's care. The thinking will only be as strong as the information base laid down in the seminary. The leader builds upon the base through further independent study and by learning from experience as the years of ministry unfold.

I once asked a colleague and a rector of a large parish to mentor a new priest. My colleague was an experienced priest and earned a PhD in biblical studies. Before agreeing to be a mentor, my colleague asked, "Does this person need work in the New Testament? I need the priest who already knows the basics taught in seminary. I don't want to spend our time together offering remedial work in the Bible. I anticipate that, in the mentoring relationship, we will integrate the academic foundation of biblical studies into ministry. In this parish, I can offer many learning experiences in a wide range of parish ministries." My colleague viewed mentoring as an academic study integrated into the daily practice of ministry and not as reviewing material that was covered in seminary. I thought, "I wish I had twenty more mentors like this!"

Academic study is the crucial foundation. Seminaries provide students with the concepts and the critical thinking to fulfill a spiritual leader's responsibility to think theologically. The academic foundation takes place within community, worship, and service. Seminaries are concerned with intellectual formation and the whole person, as students experience different aspects of the church. Students serve in parishes and other institutions, practicing preaching, pastoral care, and more. Students learn alongside accomplished priests, liturgists, and musicians of the church in the seminary's worshipping community. Faculty mentor students in groups and individually. These are the strengths that a seminary can provide to launch a spiritual leader. To assume that seminaries carry the entire responsibility for what a spiritual leader learns minimizes what seminaries do well.

What seminaries cannot change is the stage of ministry—a student is a student. Students devote most of their time to classroom study with an expert in that field. Practical classes and hands-on experience are a relatively small part of a seminary curriculum. A seminary cannot and should not be expected to do both academic preparation and practice because ministry practice cannot fully begin until the student stage concludes and the initial stage of ministry begins!

In other words, to practice ministry, the spiritual leader needs to be actively engaged in spiritual leadership. When a student moves from serving in a parish on Sunday morning and returning to academic life on Monday, some practical experience is gained. However, a Sunday field placement cannot replicate the day-to-day reality of parish ministry once a new priest is fully embedded in congregational life. In that context, there is no shifting of roles, no picking up or putting down the work of a priest. Such sustained, immersive experience cannot—and should not—be expected of seminaries to create. Learning from experts through information and content exchange differs from learning through personal reflection. Yes, you did not learn that in seminary, and there was no possible way you could have learned it there.

In the initial stage of ministry, a whole new set of priorities, challenges, dynamics, people, celebrations, and gifts emerge. Learning through the action-reflection-consider new actions-test new action model (also known experiential learning or adult learning) is used because the learner is now an autonomous adult, rather than a student learning from an expert. To learn, the adult learner must engage fully with the present moment. They draw on concepts from their knowledge base and put them to practice. The resulting actions become the focus of reflection so that the adult learner—ideally supported by a mentor, peers, and a learning congregation—can attend to self, others, God, feeling, and history at that moment.

For example, questions of reflective practice incorporate the connection to self, others, and God. "How was God present?" could be asked. "What could have frightened the person so deeply?" could also be asked, as well as "Why did you feel frightened too?" Then, with reflection, the spiritual leader creates a new action to test: "What do you want to do differently next time?" and gains new knowledge about their ministry practice. This type of learning requires absolute immersion in their practice. Reflective practice is learning what a spiritual leader was not supposed to learn in seminary and could not learn in seminary. Reflective practice is an adult learner using what she or he already knows and adding to that experience from the context of each day to grow, to build competence, and to gain confidence in ministry practice.

"I did not learn that in seminary!" is a comment we can *stop* using. Seminary and academic training necessarily come before immersion in the practice of ministry and intentional learning through reflection. The student stage comes before the initial stage of ministry, the spiritual leadership of ordained or lay people whom Jesus calls friends. The student stage is learning content from experts. The initial ministry stage is learning as an autonomous adult through reflective practice. It is not an either-or, either seminary or adult learning with reflective practice. It is both an academic study and a reflective practice.

Some might suggest that there are practical topics a seminary could teach, such as stewardship or budget preparation. I would respond that, unlike the enduring foundations of the Bible, theology, and ethics, stewardship and budget preparation can be learned more effectively in the contexts in which they are used. A stewardship process in one congregation does not always mirror that in other congregations. People continually adapt to meet the needs of their communities. The same is true for budgets. The core information is the same, but no two budgets will look the same. Each parish often has its own definition of what goes into a given line item.

Stewardship information and budget information can be shared during the early years of practice, allowing the spiritual leader to apply and practice with the information as they receive it. This underscores the importance of the mentoring programs, which also address essential topics such as stewardship and financial management. These early-stage immersion programs embody a both-and approach to learning, integrating practical experience with guided reflection.

A word of caution. I recognize that the models of seminary education are changing. Some will be three-year residential programs. For some, there is a need for and value in training priests locally, in learning environments beyond three-year residential programs. I also appreciate that online models are possible. As theological educators, learners, students, academics, and emerging priests test models, I caution against our human tendency to categorize academic formation as either residential or online. The challenge is to find the ways that allow students studying for ministry to be truly students wrestling with big, life-changing ideas within themselves and with others in a student community, and not isolated brains taking in information. Navigating the unknown ahead means creating those learning environments and learning communities while resisting the temptation to assume that seminary education must include everything a spiritual leader needs.

Seminaries and Reflective Practice

It seems to me that a seminary could be an ideal environment to introduce reflective practice. As chapter 3 describes, reflection is a cultivated form of awareness, of consciousness. This aligns with the contemplative side of the Christian tradition, practicing Centering Prayer and meditation, studying the mystics, meeting with a spiritual director to reflect on one's journey with God and growth in life in Christ. One can ask: "How does a contemplative practice of prayer begin to shape a reflective practice of ministry?" Students might consult their spiritual director to discern which questions they should ask themselves as they enter their first year of ministry.

One of the important tasks is maintaining a spiritual life after graduating from the academy or another formal program. Often, the formal academic programs focus on public worship and daily prayer in chapel. Concerning the individual, contemplative relationship with God, what questions or exercises could serve as a bridge from earlier explorations with a spiritual director to more focused reflection on specific ministry action, as an individual or in a group? How would a mentor and a new priest build a relationship so that the mentoring relationship draws on the strengths of spiritual direction and reflective learning, and so that the reflective learning in mentoring develops new dimensions for discussion with the spiritual director?

Seminaries in collaboration with bishops might also launch postgraduate learning communities for clergy. The content of these programs depends, of course, on the stage of ministry. Those in the Initial Years of Ministry have the steepest learning curve in terms of experience and content. Peer learning communities, supported by trained mentors, help new priests navigate the flood of information in their first years, develop their ministerial identity, and transition into a new community, to name just a few areas of focus. Elsewhere in this book, especially chapter 4, I describe the rich yet rapid pace of experiential learning for new priests.

There is also complementary content. Parish finances, governance, volunteer engagement, and human and facilities resource management are all new areas for a priest beginning ministry and entering parish leadership for the first time. Programs that establish habits of reflective practice and experiential learning in peer groups—paired with timely, parish-focused ministry content—provide new clergy with curated support throughout their first two years. Experienced priests and trained mentors guide peer discussions and offer deeper, one-to-one conversations that help ground these early experiences in practical wisdom.

Ideally, the bishops would collaborate with the seminary and send new priests from their diocese to such a program. The bishop might provide his or her overarching vision for the formation of priests and could advise on topics that new priests really need. Enrolling in this program means that the program would be beneficial to the priest, the diocese, and the bishop. The seminary's role is more straightforward since the seminary already knows how to recruit qualified instructors and determine the best way to deliver that material. Recruiting teachers and the facilities, virtual or in-person classrooms, are resources few bishops have. Some collaborations like this between bishops and seminaries already exist.

Sending new priests from the diocese to a fee-based program is also an important form of collaboration. I am assuming this postgraduate program is fee-based simply because the necessary resources require financial support. When launching a new program, it is essential to build in a funding model from the outset. Typically, this involves securing a grant specifically intended to support the ongoing formation of clergy.

The grant often requires the applicant to outline a sustainability plan. Once the program is underway, designers must also demonstrate how it will continue operating without grant funding. The bishop's ongoing participation in sending seminarians and priests to this fee-based program is essential to ensuring continued support for the clergy.

I recognize that not every diocese has the resources to pay fees for its priests' continuing education. The seminary or other organization needs financial resources to offer these programs. And the financial resources across all dioceses are not equal. What are the partnerships yet to be developed that could support the diocese with fewer resources? Is there a way to share resources among dioceses by forming a consortium or an intentional ministry for the Initial Years of Ministry? My wish is that bishops would form a peer group—one that could reflect together in order to generate a range of possible actions to address the support needs of all new clergy.

Most often, when funds are unavailable or a bishop believes that the priests in her diocese need something different from the program's content, the diocese creates local programs with dedicated, experienced local clergy. Most clergy want to be helpful, but as parish priests, many do not have the time or skills to mentor, teach, listen, facilitate, and administer a learning community.

In addition, new clergy are especially reluctant to be candid with priests in the diocese whom they do not know well. They recognize that a future colleague could be hearing very personal struggles. Just as every adult does, new clergy want to be seen as competent. That person working with them today could be deciding a job for them tomorrow. Clergy seldom move beyond surface-level disclosure when engaging with their own diocesan staff or colleagues. They are generally more comfortable discussing what they don't know in group contexts or with mentors from other dioceses.

Bishops and a seminary collaborating to offer a post-graduate experiential learning community need not be limited to the Initial Years of Ministry. As chapter 4 shows, ministry unfolds in distinct stages. Peer-based cohorts guided by a mentor can support clergy in the six-to-ten-year range, those with more than fifteen years of experience, or clergy preparing to design, plan, and launch a significant new ministry. All of these are viable possibilities.

Peer groups can be organized around a shared ministry context, such as the challenges faced by smaller congregations. Over the years, conferences and regular gatherings have brought together priests who are wrestling with similar ministry questions. These events often generate valuable ideas and offer practical strategies. Yet the underlying learning model tends to be more pedagogical in nature. As a result, clergy and lay leaders typically return home, implementing only portions of what they encountered at the conference.

In all this, I am advocating for continuous adult learning, the substance of which is immediate experience. The mentors and peer groups are the support framework to keep the learning flowing.

A seminary has the resources to construct the framework. The bishop has experience with priests to guide content and keep the framework in working order by sending priests from the diocese.

Such programs have been thoroughly tested. Over the past twenty-five years, grants, seminaries, dioceses, and congregations have explored various models for clergy to learn in context. My primary involvement has been with grants for new clergy programs. Among these efforts, the program that most closely engaged contextual learning for new clergy consisted of twenty-four congregation-based initiatives and called Transition into Ministry. In the initial Transition into Ministry program created by Lilly Endowment Inc., the core model resembled a medical residency: participants were called "clergy residents," and the host churches were designated as "teaching congregations."

The congregations chosen to receive the grant funds had a wide range of parish ministry experiences, so the new clergy would have the most varied formative experiences. Again, like a medical residency, the intent was to develop congregations where new clergy could experience ministry practice and then serve the wider church, prepared with a solid foundation of academics and integrated practice. The congregation understood their role as forming these clergy to be pastors in any congregational context. Over time, the congregations would develop new funding sources to sustain the program.

Today, five of the original twenty-four congregations still have programs in place. For the most part, these five congregations raised the funds to endow the programs. The most expensive line item in a clergy residency program is the clergy salary. Few congregations can afford to add two, three, or four staff members to their budgets. However, the idea spread to new congregations. Including the original five, the Teaching Congregations with Clergy Residency programs number twenty-one. The idea spread primarily among Baptist churches but also includes Lutheran, Presbyterian, and United Church of Christ congregations. Within The Episcopal Church, one congregation continues with the clergy residency model. These programs begin the habit of reflective practice and support continuous learning.

Other models have also been tested. For new clergy, one model concentrated the academic curriculum of the MDiv in the first two years and expanded hours in the third year in participating congregations that were trained to be Teaching Congregations. These programs were less successful because shifting the academic schedule became uneven.

For experienced clergy, tested programs include seminary-based mentor training and peer learning groups organized around a stage or context in ministry. In these programs, some examples of peer groups are rectors in parishes with schools, episcopal school chaplains, and women clergy seeking executive leadership. Not by design, many of these grant programs launched during the COVID-19 pandemic. The cohorts with which I am familiar effectively addressed the needs for collegiality, learning from peers, and building skills.

Seminary-diocese collaborations are also currently being tested. One seminary has developed a program that assembles peer groups of new clergy selected by their bishops, provides opening and closing retreats, delivers essential early ministry content, and offers weekly one-on-one mentoring for each participant. Except for the in-person opening and closing retreats, the program is conducted virtually. Its aim is to create a dynamic mix of clergy and mentors drawn from multiple dioceses.

Establishing a habit of reflective practice, claiming adult autonomy for learning, learning from direct experience, and growing personally, professionally, and vocationally are all possible when existing resources are leveraged effectively.

"I did not learn that in seminary!" Yes, you did not learn that in seminary and that is great. Thanks be to God that the academy uses its resources well, teaching the core theological curriculum and providing pastoral formation in community. Thanks be to God that local learning and hybrid programs use their resources effectively to deliver the core curriculum of theological study and formation within their local or hybrid communities. Thanks be to God that bishops understand the significance of integrating academic learning and ministry practice, especially for new clergy, and that they send them to programs best equipped to offer that support. Now let's celebrate this next stage of ministry with its own style of learning: adult learning through reflective practice, mentoring, peers, and learning congregations for the benefit of the spiritual leader and the church.

CHAPTER 7
Conclusion

A ship is safe in the harbor, but that is not what ships are built for.

—John A. Shedd[1]

With this book, we have slipped across the water from our familiar beach of self, others, and God. We have transported ourselves to a distant point we set on the horizon by using reflective practice with mentors, peers, and learning congregations. Like all voyages, the conditions are anticipated and yet cannot be predicted. Along the way, puffs of breeze, changes of tide, a gust of wind, mistakes in reading the condition, or technique, such as not enough sail pulled in or too much sail let out, change our course so that our corrections are part of the journey. We can feel the changes in conditions, and even if our first course correction is a mistake, we can always make another correction because the wind, sail, and boat showed us what did and did not work.

How many times we need to make corrections determines our Momentum. Lots of corrections, and we will

1. John A. Shedd, *Salt from My Attic* (Mosher Press, 1928).

not travel very far, very fast. Reading conditions and using them to the best benefit of the boat, sail, and the captain's skill keep the boat moving in a straight line. Then we will travel as fast as the wind and our skills allow.

The amazing thing about sailing is that if the captain is paying attention, her skill is always improving. Each change presents an opportunity for new information. Tweak the rudder to the right, and the boat goes left. Pull in the sail a little tighter in a stiff breeze, and the boat speeds up.

Only so much learning about sailing happens on shore. Learning to sail means getting in the boat with the wind. The same is true for the practice of ministry. It is the both-and of on-shore learning and on-the-water learning. Academic training and the practice of ministry.

A caution about sailing is that the surprises in conditions can take you to the edge of your ability. Then your heart is pounding, and your mind is racing to think of another tactic to try before the boat capsizes. The more capsizes you go through, the fewer you will have in the same weather conditions. Then, you seek the challenge of tougher conditions. Many sailors relish the thrill and the ability to improve.

Another caution about sailing is that it can be perfect. Warm, just enough breeze, a glide along cool water on a hot, hot summer day. No place else to be. What is not to like? (Well, you need to like water and sun.) In those moments, you wonder why you don't do this all the time. However, no sail stays perfect. There are always surprises. It's a mix.

The same is true of ministry practice. There are surprises that take you to the edge of your ability. Your heart is pounding, and your mind is racing. Big surprises in ministry are not what I call thrilling because they are often due to great tragedy or misconduct. Yet it can be thrilling to be at the edge and know that as you make the best decision you can in the moment, a mentor, a peer group, or a safe friend will be there to reflect with you.

And there is no perfect congregation or ministry. Know that a mentor, peer, or safe friend is there to reflect with you. Know that you are always in a loving, growing, deep relationship of friendship with Jesus and in Jesus. The joys of these experiences are as important as the surprises. It is all the practice of ministry as we prepare to navigate the unknown.

APPENDIX
Reflective Practice Guide for Stages of Ministry—The Initial Year

In the left-hand column of the chart below are examples of common learning goals for the Initial Years of Ministry. When using this chart, you may use the examples and add your own. The second column from the left identifies areas of learning, growth, and improvement. For example, "I am finding my preaching voice" is a felt sense that, as you experience growing competence in preaching, you will also experience more flexibility for expressing yourself. It is analogous to the more an author writes, the greater sense the author has of her own voice. The next five columns are ways for you to assess yourself. This is your subjective measure. Completing this reflective practice guide over time, you can see what changes. Inviting a mentor and/or a peer group to be part of the process expands the perspectives on your own learning.

This guide is an example of one of the resources Soul Assets Consulting offers.

	Initial Year	Yes, definitely	Yes, sometimes	Yes, but rarely	No, not yet	Not sure
Preaching preparation & practice finding my voice	I prepare and practice my sermons. I am discovering my peaching voice through my writing and delivery. I try out different methods of delivery.					
Sacramental leadership practice in the rite preparation and planning	I am aware of all the "first time" of celebrating sacraments. As a "first" I practice the rite. I allow adequate time for preparation and planning.					
parish finance & facilities	I smoothly administer the basics of parish infrastructure.					

	Initial Year	Yes, definitely	Yes, sometimes	Yes, but rarely	No, not yet	Not sure
balance time for parish & personal	I try out different ways to arrange my schedule. I am flexible to adjust between parish and personal time. I feel obligated to put parish needs first.					
Pastoral Care & new relationships	I am forming positive relationships throughout the congregation.					
Integrating spiritual practices & personal theology into current context	I am transferring my regular spiritual practices from seminary into a personal practice for life the parish. I am integrating academic concepts into daily parish ministry. My piety and the parish's practices are aligned.					

Strengths:

Areas for development:

ACKNOWLEDGMENTS

Over the past twenty-six years of mentoring clergy, I had the privilege of wonderful relationships and thoughtful conversations. Each one shaped my thoughts and ideas. It is not possible to thank everyone who sailed along with me.

Thank you to the Lilly Endowment Inc., especially Craig Dystrak and Chris Coble, for their inspiration and guidance during the initial Transition into Ministry program (TiM) and beyond; to my colleagues and innovation partners—George Mason, Peter Marty, Jim Wind, and David Wood. Craig and Jim now rest with the saints of light. Their work created the conditions to urge the church to intentionally care for her clergy. To Pierce Klemmt, rector of Christ Church Alexandria, VA, where we worked on the first TiM grant, to the clergy residents courageous enough to enter an innovative program promising to build "holy habits and healthy leadership practices," to Ken Knapp who wrote the initial grant in 1999 and consistently supported the program, to the people of Christ Church Alexandria who intuitively understood the significance of forming new clergy for the future of the church and embraced becoming a teaching congregation.

Thank you to all who engaged in the mentoring grants and conversations that followed, especially to the mentors of Berkeley Divinity School at Yale's Virtual Curacy program.

I am also privileged to call former mentees colleagues, especially Laura Gettys, Jenni Ovenstone, Cathy Rafferty Quinn, and Mpho Tutu Van Feurth.

Thank you to the parishes of The Episcopal Church of the Redeemer and The Episcopal Church of the Holy Trinity as participants in the Connecting Conversations model and as enthusiastic supporters.

Thank you to my colleagues in the Diocese of Long Island, especially the coaches who are a peer learning community for skill development and peer supervision, and to those in the Initial Years of Ministry program.

And my deep gratitude to my colleagues, Chilton Knudsen, George Mason, and Pamela Mott, who read drafts of this manuscript with helpful suggestions and support to keep going.

When I started a part-time position in September 2000 at Christ Church Alexandria as the Program Director of Transition into Ministry, I could not have known that I was discovering a new passion in ministry. I am grateful for all who continue to be on this journey with me.

SUGGESTED READING

The Heart of Centering Prayer Non Dual Christianity in Theory and in Practice by Cynthia Bourgeault.

Transitions: Making Sense of Life's Changes 2nd edition by William Bridges.

Dare to Lead: Brave Work. Tough Conversations. Whole Hearts. by Brené Brown.

Generation to Generation: Family Process in Church and in Synagogue by Edwin H. Friedman.

A Failure of Nerve: Leadership in the Age of the Quick Fix by Edwin H. Friedman.

The Practice of Adaptive Leadership: Tools and Tactics for Changing Your Organization by Ronald A. Heifetz.

Wherever You Go There You Are: Mindfulness Meditation in Everyday Life by Jon Kabat Zinn.

Open Mind, Open Hearts: The Contemplative Dimension of the Gospel 20th Anniversary Edition by Thomas Keating.

Self-Compassion: The Proven Power of Being Kind to Yourself by Kirstin Neff, PhD.

The Reflective Practitioner: How Professionals Think in Action by Donald A Schön.

BIBLIOGRAPHY

The Book of Common Prayer and Administration of the Sacraments and Other Rites and Ceremonies of the Church. According to the use of The Episcopal Church. Church Publishing Incorporated, 1979.

Brown, Brené. *Dare to Lead: Brave Work. Tough Conversations. Whole Hearts.* Random House Books, 2018.

Butler, Hannah. "Understanding the Territory of Reflective Practice." In *Creating the Reflective Habit: A Practical Guide for Coaches, Mentors, and Leaders*, by Michelle Lucas, 4-6. Routledge, 2023.

Contemplativeoutreach.org. Accessed 2026.

Gallup.com. https://www.gallup.com/cliftonstrengths.

Holleman, Heather. *The Six Conversations: Pathways to Connecting in an Age of Isolation and Incivility.* Moody Publishers, 2022.

Kabat Zinn, Jon. *Full Catastrophe Living: Using the Wisdom of Your Body and Mind to Face Stress, Illness, and Pain.* Bantam Books, 2013.

Keating, Thomas. *Open Minds, Open Hearts 20th Anniversary Edition.* Bloomsbury Continuum, 2006.

Knowles, Malcolm S., Holton III, Elwood F, and Swanson, Richard A. *The Adult Learner The Definitive*

Classic in Adult Education and Human Resource Development 5th Edition. Butter-Heinemann, 1998.

Kolb, David A. *Experiential Learning Experience as the Source of Learning and Development.* Pearson Education, Inc., 2015.

Lucas, Michelle. *Creating the Reflective Habit: A Practical Guide for Coaches, Mentors, and Leaders.* Routledge, 2023.

Neff, Kristin. *Fierce Self Compassion: How to Harness Kindness to Speak Up, Claim Your Power, and Thrive.* Harper, 2021.

Neff, Kristin and Christopher, Germer. *The Mindful Self-Compassion Workbook: A Proven Way to Accept Yourself, Build Inner Strength, and Thrive.* The Guildford Press, 2021.

Salzberg, Sharon. *Open to Life: Learning to Love Yourself and the World.* Macmillan Audio, 2021.

Schön, Donald A. *The Reflective Practitioner: How Professionals Think in Action.* Basic Books, 1983.

Scott, Susan. *Fierce Conversations: Achieving Success at Work and in Life One Conversation at a Time.* Berkley Books, 2004.

INDEX

www.ingramcontent.com/pod-product-compliance
Ingram Content Group UK Ltd.
Pitfield, Milton Keynes, MK11 3LW, UK
UKHW051834030926
8393IPUK00004B/42

9 781640 658806